Journey
to the
Afterlife

To Write to the Author

If you wish to contact the author or would like more information about this book, please write to the author in care of Llewellyn Worldwide Ltd. and we will forward your request. Both the author and publisher appreciate hearing from you and learning of your enjoyment of this book and how it has helped you. Llewellyn Worldwide Ltd. cannot guarantee that every letter written to the author can be answered, but all will be forwarded. Please write to:

Kristy Robinett
℅ Llewellyn Worldwide
2143 Wooddale Drive
Woodbury, MN 55125-2989

Please enclose a self-addressed stamped envelope for reply,
or $1.00 to cover costs. If outside the USA, enclose
an international postal reply coupon.

Many of Llewellyn's authors have websites with additional
information and resources. For more information,
please visit our website at www.llewellyn.com

Journey
to the
Afterlife

Comforting
Messages & Lessons
from Loved Ones in Spirit

KRISTY ROBINETT

Llewellyn Publications
Woodbury, Minnesota

FIRST EDITION
First Printing, 2018

Cover design by Shira Atakpu
Editing by Brian R. Erdrich

Llewellyn Publications is a registered trademark of Llewellyn Worldwide Ltd.

Library of Congress Cataloging-in-Publication Data
Names: Robinett, Kristy, author.
　Title: Journey to the afterlife : comforting messages & lessons from loved
　　ones in spirit / Kristy Robinett.
　Description: First edition. | Woodbury, Minnesota : Llewellyn Publications,
　　2018. | Includes bibliographical references.
　Identifiers: LCCN 2018014969 (print) | LCCN 2018022406 (ebook) | ISBN
　　9780738755472 (ebook) | ISBN 9780738752693 (alk. paper)
　Subjects: LCSH: Future life. | Spiritualism.
　Classification: LCC BF1311.F8 (ebook) | LCC BF1311.F8 R6325 2018 (print) |
　　DDC 133.9—dc23
　LC record available at https://lccn.loc.gov/2018014969

Llewellyn Worldwide Ltd. does not participate in, endorse, or have any authority
or responsibility concerning private business transactions between our authors
and the public.
　All mail addressed to the author is forwarded but the publisher cannot, unless
specifically instructed by the author, give out an address or phone number.
　Any internet references contained in this work are current at publication time,
but the publisher cannot guarantee that a specific location will continue to be
maintained. Please refer to the publisher's website for links to authors' websites
and other sources.

Llewellyn Publications
A Division of Llewellyn Worldwide Ltd.
2143 Wooddale Drive
Woodbury, MN 55125-2989
www.llewellyn.com

Printed in the United States of America

Other Books by Kristy Robinett

Forevermore

It's a Wonderful Afterlife

Messenger Between Worlds

Tails from the Afterlife

Dedication

To all of those on the other side who trusted in me to share their experiences in heaven, hell, and in between.

Contents

Acknowledgments

Since I could first start reading, books were my best friend, my escape, my excuse to cry, my outlet to laugh, love, and find adventure. I picked up a pen early on and began writing poetry and short stories, hardly sharing them except for a few assignments in English class. I have a learning disability similar to dyslexia. Instead of flipping letters around, I flip sentence syntax. In my mind I see it in the correct manner, but on paper or screen it reads like Yoda. It wasn't classified as a learning disability until I was in college. When teachers would ask or assign a paper on what I wanted to be when I grew up, I rarely hesitated to tell them I wanted to be an author. It was often met with criticism and an offer of another career direction. I was, however, determined to write no matter what, and so I wrote. I wrote for magazines and blogs and became a content writer for webpages. My gratitude goes out to Llewellyn for taking a chance on me, and Amy Glaser, who inspires me daily to reach for my dreams and who believes in me even after I have read, reread, and then read what I wrote out loud, only for it to still be Yoda-like and need to be corrected. And also to Brian R. Erdrich for helping to catch my mistakes, suggesting edits, and making me feel like a real author.

To the continued support and unconditional love of my husband, Chuck Robinett, and my children, Micaela Even Kempf, Connor Even, Cora Kutnick, and Molly Robinett.

To my dad, Ron Schiller, who keeps me laughing even when frustrated, and my mom-in-law, Mary Lou, who always has a story to tell and wisdom to give.

Love to my brother, Duane Schiller, and my sister, Cheri Ford, for dad-sitting when I have to go out of town.

Several years back a couple came to a library event I was presenting in. My husband and I met up with them afterward and they've been our best friends since. Mikey and Marjanna McClain, our travel buddies, who so lovingly help us with events, late-night laughs, and constant adventures—I can only hope we have decades of more fun.

To Mary Byberg, my assistant and friend who's so patient with my clients and most of all with me.

To my best friends and confidantes: Gayle Buchan, Donna Shorkey, and Jenni Licata. Thank you to Colleen Kwiecinski and her mad Cooper sitting skills. Courtney Sieira for being the best hair counselor around. To Jan Tomes, Kathy Curatolo, and Ryan Sparks for their friendship and help with events. SUP.

And finally, I thank the thousands of clients and their loved ones on the other side who have touched my life more than I could ever eloquently communicate. For their stories and the connections that never get old. Everyday I'm grateful and feel blessed.

Disclaimer

Although the stories are real-life occurrences, some names and identifying details have been changed to protect the privacy of individuals.

Introduction

Since I was three years old I've had spirits visiting me, telling me their life and death stories, woes and celebrations. As much as I tried to shut down the afterlife lines, the connection was never broken. Now that I'm in my, well, let's just say forty-somethings, that line of spirits continues. When I was younger I would throw the blankets over my head and wish them away, but today I listen to them. The line resembles the DMV on most nights, and there are times I'm overwhelmed and overly exhausted with life, then come home and have to deal with the afterlife too. After resisting my calling for years, I embraced it and became a spiritual counselor to the living, along with the dead. To be honest, there are times I find the dead more fascinating.

I don't have the ability to channel like Whoopi Goldberg from the movie *Ghost*. To me that's just creepy, plus I'm too much of a control freak to allow a spirit snatcher to do a takeover. I actually see spirits as if they are flesh and blood, standing right in front of me, the way they were before their physical body died. I communicate with spirits, typically telepathically, and I feel their emotions and the physical pain they felt in life. For the longest time I felt cursed being able to see, hear, and feel that which was beyond my own senses.

Fifteen years ago I decided to stop drinking the negativity and considered the connections as a blessing instead. I like to take a glass-half-full approach, and I am thankful that I didn't get the "blessing" where my face distorts and I start to talk in tongues. I'm comfortable with admitting I'm a scaredy-cat. If the spirits looked like anything Hollywood depicts as ghosts or spirits, I would more than likely not have embraced my gift at all. Seriously, I'm the girl who has to keep a nightlight on in her bedroom, to the dismay of my husband, and although I lead paranormal investigations in the scariest of places, I have my flashlight and sage ready in case anyone jumps out at me. Just a side note on that: I'm sensible and I know that neither the flashlight nor the sage will help me, but it's my security blanket anyhow.

Everyone has their escape. Some go to a beach, others to a spa, while another might go to the gym, a bookstore, or even a bar. Ever since I was old enough to wander off with my bicycle my escape was the cemetery. Just a mile from my home, down the busy Detroit, Michigan road, was over 150 acres of peace just past the ornate iron gates. With a serene river and plenty of wildlife, it was my secret haven. I respected the grave sites, simply finding a spot to sit where I fed the birds and squirrels, and would often pull a journal out of my backpack to write in or a mystery or romance novel to gobble up, depending upon my mood. I cried over fights with friends, contemplated crushes, and even took one of my first driving lessons with my dad down the windy roads. Not once was I ever bothered by a spirit there. When I got into high school I told a new friend about my hideaway. "Aren't you afraid?" she responded, horrified. I was never once afraid in that cemetery. "It's the living that scare me most," I'd tell her, but I was only telling her a half truth. It wouldn't be until now that I spill the other half.

Being raised Lutheran, attending parochial school, I was taught that heaven was up toward the sky, in the land of the clouds. I was taught that hell was down below, and if you weren't baptized, didn't go to church, committed suicide, or pretty much weren't a Lutheran, that was the place you went. I was taught purgatory was something Catholics made up in order to give people an out. I was taught God judged, Satan ruled, and that there wasn't a gray area. Then there I was seeing, hearing, feeling, sensing, and communicating with spirits who were telling me firsthand accounts of their afterlife and it was hardly anything like what I had been told.

Every birth, life, and death offer experiences and lessons through the losses and the gains. I'm here to share the stories of what happens next according to several of the spirits who've visited me once their physical bodies died. Just as every birth story is different, so is every death, and so is every one's afterlife. These are the stories they've asked to be shared. These are their experiences in heaven, hell, and in between.

Part One

Heaven

The journey to heaven has been told by many who've had near death experiences. Some have spoken of a long stairway, others a bright light, and others were simply whisked to another location. Many skeptics have discounted these experiences as nothing more than hallucinations, but for the experiencers it was real, true, and life-changing.

For most experiencers, they describe a timelessness that flows naturally. There's no clock, there's no need to be on a schedule, and future preparations are irrelevant, as it's just the now. The now isn't met with stressful expectations that our life here holds; instead it's joyful and calm, something that isn't easily replicated on earth.

In 2008 Dr. Eben Alexander fell into a coma after his brain was attacked by a rare illness. He shared his near-death-experience in his book *Proof of Heaven*. "I was in a place of clouds. Big, puffy, pink-white ones that showed up sharply against the deep blue-black sky," he said. "A sound, huge and booming like a glorious

chant, came down from above, and I wondered if the winged beings were producing it. Again thinking about it later, it occurred to
me that the joy of these creatures, as they soared along, was such
that they *had* to make this noise—that if the joy didn't come out of
them this way then they would simply not otherwise be able to
contain it."

Dr. Mary Neal, an orthopedic spine surgeon, says she visited
heaven after drowning in 1999 after a kayaking accident. "The
senses were different. I mean, the beauty was incredibly intense;
there's no other earthly experience that is equivalent." Mary says
she did not see a tunnel of light; rather, she saw something much
more expansive. "But I was in a hurry to get to this big, domed
structure of sorts," she says. "There were many spirits inside, and
when I arrived, they were overjoyed and welcoming me and greeting me and really joyful at my arrival" (Neal 2012).

The beings that cared for her wore robes and exuded a vibration filled with love and joy; Mary didn't want to leave. The spiritual beings told her that it wasn't her time and she was to share her
story with others. Before her return, though, they shared with her
a future incident that would involve the passing of her son. She returned to her body and reunited with her friends and family in
hopes of changing the course of the prediction. But she was unsuc-
cessful, and ten years later her eldest son was hit by a car and killed.

If you ask a handful of people what they want their heaven to
be like, you'll get a handful of answers. Some may find living in the
hustle and bustle of a cityscape to be heavenly, while some may
find that hellish. Others want to be surrounded by fields of lavender and wild horses, and some may feel that to be torturous. Some
want to be with family and friends; others feel at peace in their own

solitude. A cat in your lap or a dog by your side may feel calming, but to another it's misery.

Ernest Hemingway described his heaven in a letter he wrote to F. Scott Fitzgerald. "To me a heaven would be a big bull ring with me holding two Barrera seats and a trout stream outside that no one else was allowed to fish in and two lovely houses in the town," the letter read (Grunwald 1999).

Close your eyes and visualize a place where you can be in the now. For some it's a beach, others it's the forest, some it's a casino, and yet others it's actually their workplace. Heaven has been described by my many spirit encounters as passing through a veil where your physical pain disappears and your soul is given the opportunity to find peace, joy, and happiness. Your senses are heightened, you're understood, and there's a fountain of continuous love that surrounds and cradles your soul. It's the perfect earth, but not real and tangible like this earth. There are no problems, sins, betrayals, jealousies, or comparisons.

Close your eyes and envision the most beautiful sunset, sunrise, deep and true relationship, or belly laugh. Imagine your favorite scent, your favorite food, your favorite memory, your favorite vacation. Those glimpses of experiences are tiny tastes of what heaven is.

Death is not a wall; death is a doorway. The relocation to heaven isn't just one place; it is your place. So wish big, and believe in your heaven.

Chapter One

Children and the Afterlife

None of us escape death. When life has fulfilled its purpose, we cross into the next threshold. Death brings liberation, a freedom to be the purest form you were meant to be on earth that may have been bogged down with earthly anchors.

It's so easy to celebrate the birth of a baby, and so easy to cry when the child is taken into the afterlife. The interesting thing is that the afterlife rejoices when they receive that soul back. Birthdays and death days are one in the same on the other side. They are both celebrations. Here on earth, we feel death is a cheat, a loss, and something horrific.

Nobody likes to lose anything, except for maybe weight. Losing something that is loved and dear is terrible and often can't be emotionally accepted. I admit that even though I see the celebrations on the other side after a passing, when I'm dealing with a child that was transferred to heaven, I can't help but feel the sadness and loss as well. Even though I know they are fine, and I can pass along that message, it is still so difficult. When my uncle passed away, my mom said, "No parent should ever have to bury their child," and it is a long-standing belief that I have as well. The cold reality of it is that it happens.

The Loss of a Child

Losing a child is never easy. An array of feelings goes into that loss, as with every loss. The soul of the lost doesn't hold on to the sadness, anger, or regret, nor do they carry that with them back if they do choose to reincarnate.

For me, children are the easiest to communicate with on the other side. They are excited to share their heaven and happiness, and attempt to knock down the walls of grief that so often build up around their loved ones left here. If the child passed before speaking age, I often have a family member or spirit guide with them aiding in their communication. Fortunately, on most occasions the spirit child is able to communicate despite the walls of grief and despair built around the parents.

Children easily forgive, easily understand instruction, and easily progress. They aren't bogged down with the conflict that many adults hold close to them like treasures; in fact, these conflicts are remnants of hurt that should've been trashed long ago. Children know how to let go and love without prejudice, both on earth and in the afterlife. They are our touch of heaven.

Many times a child that is lost has already lived many lifetimes before and therefore they understand that their death is simply a transition into a new beginning. They are often more brave and mature, and are met by spirit people, who although they may have not met in an earthly sense, they have known from the spirit world.

Some may be from soul connections in past lives, and some may be connected to the souls of their parents that they have never met on earth. The greeting in heaven for a child is one of the most beautiful things I've ever witnessed. They are guided by archangels, angels, guides, and many others who are attracted to their individual vibrancy.

Winnie

Winnie was a spirited child from birth, coming into the world at three in the morning with only an hour of labor. Her parents, Maya and Tom, joked that it was a foretelling of how her life would be—hurried. She was an overachiever from the beginning, excelling in every mark. She gained weight like a champ, crawled and walked before her peers, and talked in sentences when she was two years old. Of course, every parent thinks their child is a genius, but Winnie wasn't just smart, she was wise.

"Maya, I have to commend you for your vibrant daughter," Winnie's preschool teacher said when Maya picked her up from school.

That morning Winnie's teacher and her fiancé had had a horrible fight and, although she thought she'd hidden it well, Winnie came over at the beginning of class and asked her if she needed a hug.

"Winnie, just go and color," the teacher snapped.

"No, I think you need a hug," Winnie said and, without asking, wrapped her arms around her teacher's legs. "It's going to be okay. Heaven makes it that way."

Winnie's teacher looked down as if she was just hugged by heaven. She thanked Winnie, who was already skipping away to color a picture.

"Thank you for this gift," Winnie's teacher praised.

Maya was humbled, but not surprised. Winnie had always picked up on the emotions of others and was sensitive to her environment.

———

It was a month after Winnie's fourth birthday when Maya woke up to find Winnie lethargic and feverish.

"Let's get you up and take a bath," she mothered.

Winnie could usually walk, but when Maya tried to help her stand up Winnie screamed in a pain Maya had never heard before.

"Tom, meet me at the hospital," she texted her husband. "Maya can't stand."

———

The doctors knew immediately what it was, but obviously required further testing. A couple days later it was confirmed that Winnie had a cancerous tumor on her brain that she probably had since birth, but as she grew it grew also.

"What now?" Winnie's parents asked the doctors, trying to stay hopeful.

The doctors weren't hopeful, though, and said they could try surgery, but they doubted it would help and would just be painful.

"Ask Winnie what she wants," one of the doctors suggested.

"Ask a four-year-old?" Tom balked. "Ask a four-year-old to make a life or death decision?"

But it wasn't a life or death decision, it was a death or death decision. Maya and Tom couldn't bear to tell their daughter what was happening, and decided to do the surgery, praying it would be a miracle. Doctors have been wrong before, haven't they? They tried to convince themselves.

They held Winnie tightly before handing her over to the surgeons. "This should make you better," they said trying to convince themselves as much as their daughter.

Winnie survived the surgery. They removed as much of the tumor as they could, but when she opened her eyes she was blind. They warned it could be permanent, but hoped it was temporary.

"Mommy," Winnie calmly called out.

"I'm right here." Maya hadn't left the hospital in the last couple weeks, constantly by her daughter's side.

"Mommy, I know that I can't see but when I get to heaven I'll be able to see and I'll give you a hug every chance I can. Okay Mommy? I'll let you know I got there okay. I promise. Let's pinky promise, Mommy. Okay?"

Maya couldn't find words, choking back her sobs. She grabbed Winnie's pinky and twisted it gently around hers, being careful to avoid pulling any of the tubes all around her little girl. An hour later Winnie fell into a medicated sleep.

"Go take a shower and get something to eat," the nurse urged Maya. "She's stable and if anything happens I'll buzz you," the nurse said, referring to the hospital pager that all the parents of critically ill children are given. Maya felt like it was a scarlet letter of sorts. A club she didn't want to be in. She nodded, kissed Maya on the forehead, and headed to the hotel that was attached to the hospital. A warm shower would hopefully clear some of her cobwebs away. She was trying to hold it together while Tom worked. He felt horribly guilty for not being there, but his employer wasn't accommodating their emergency and they had no idea how long they'd be in the hospital. They hoped and prayed that Winnie would be released into home care in a couple weeks and then things would be easier, back to normal.

Maya was changing into fresh clothes when the buzzer went off with a 911. She rushed out the door, not even certain if she closed it behind her. When she got to Winnie's room there were more medical professionals than she'd ever seen. She remembered screaming, a blood curdling "No" at the top of her lungs, knowing her baby girl was gone, she could feel it in her soul. A few nurses tried to hold her back. The doctors weren't giving up on Winnie. They didn't like to lose a patient, especially a child, but there wasn't anything else they could do. Winnie was gone.

———

Winnie loved yellow. "Why yellow?" her dad had asked her. "Why not blue, or pink, or purple?"

Winnie laughed at the silliness. "Yellow is the color of the sunshine. It's the color of spring flowers, and it makes everyone happy," she replied in all her wisdom.

Her father went up to speak of Winnie's grace and will. "She was always in a hurry," he told the three hundred funeral goers all wearing a sea of lemon yellow, Winnie's favorite color. "She was quick to be born, and quick to go back home to heaven. Everyone that met her was hugged. She was our hug from heaven. I think many of you were gifted one. I hope that as we all grieve and miss her we're reminded that selfishly we wish she was here, but I'm sure there's a reason she's there," he pointed toward the high ceilings in the church. "I just wish I knew why," he broke down.

———

As I was shopping at a local department store, the spirit of a young girl kept pulling me toward a lady she said was her mom. It's rare for me to go up to a perfect stranger and bring through a message from their loved one. Ethically I felt it was an invasion of privacy, but Winnie wasn't a "no" kind of kid, so I went against my policy and touched the lady's shoulder.

"I know this is going to sound crazy, but I have a young girl in spirit who says she's your daughter and she wants to connect with you."

"Is this a sick joke?" she said, putting her hands on her hips, tensing her shoulder.

"I promise it's not. I'm a professional medium and this is so against my policy, but your daughter is persistent. She shows me Winnie the Pooh. Maybe a favorite toy? And she says she wants you to know what her heaven is like. Can we sit down somewhere so I can share?" I offered.

The lady half nodded in suspicious agreement and we walked into the fitting room of all places and sat on the bench.

"She's good, by the way," I began. "She looks to be about eight years old."

"She was four when she died. It's been four years, though. And her name is Winnie. I'm Maya," she introduced.

"And I apologize for being rude. I'm Kristy. She was four on her passing? That makes sense then. I see children grow on the other side to the age they would've been in spirit, but still recognizable to you even if it's been twenty years."

Children can grow in the spirit. When a child shows up via mediumship, they can appear as the loved one knew them. This helps to recognize and validate who it is. They then often grow into the spirit they become on the other side.

"She says she couldn't see here, and when she fell asleep she could see and she was in front of a large water fountain like you see at the Detroit Zoo," I squinted, hoping I was interpreting that correctly.

"That was our last field trip out," Maya gasped.

"Around the fountain were all these people, so happy to see her. They were singing. She said it was so beautiful. Then she could see you crying, and she asked if she could go back. They told her that her mission there was done; she had work to do on the other side," I tried explaining.

"She has a job?"

"She says she has important chores. One of which is your mom, she's concerned about your mom."

Maya lifted her one eyebrow and curled her mouth. "My mom's fine."

"She's concerned about your mom," I repeated. "She feels that she needs to get her heart checked. Now, I'm not a medical professional, I'm simply a messenger," I explained.

Maya nodded in understanding.

"She's watching over the family, she says she playing and going to school, but not like school here. It's not about reading or writing; it's about helping and healing. And hugging. She says her job is to be a super hugger."

I smiled because I could see Winnie on the other side of the bench, sitting next to her mom. Maya kept brushing her knee, but what she was feeling was her daughter touching her.

There was a moment of contemplation. "This is crazy," the lady laughed. "But yes, Winnie was a great hugger. She hugged strangers, some of which didn't like to be hugged, but when Winnie hugged them you could see any darkness in their life just fade."

"That's what she's doing on the other side," I reassured. "She's trying to heal the darkness in people. She's also with your dad."

Maya once again gave me an odd look of doubt. "My dad is here, he's living."

"Does he have Alzheimer's?"

"He does!" she exclaimed.

"For some reason I see those with late stage Alzheimer's or late stage dementia on the other side. It's like they've escaped this world but their body hasn't caught up. She says he takes her fishing."

Maya clapped her hands together. "When dad retired that is all he did. Morning, noon, and evening. It made my mom so mad, especially since she had to clean the fish and she hated eating fish. And last week mom told me dad said he saw Winnie. We thought it was the Alzheimer's. Was it really her?"

Nodding, I continued. "Winnie says since her passing and his Alzheimer's he hasn't fished. Take him fishing one last time. You'll feel her there too," I smiled. "My husband probably thinks I'm lost in the fitting room. I have to go, but can I give you a hug from Winnie?"

Maya stood up and held out her arms as if to greet a toddler home from school. I wrapped my arms around her and we hugged for a long time. Not one tear was shed by either of us and after the hug I walked away.

Winnie was the hug healer, and although I went against policy, I think I needed that hug just as much as Maya.

The Afterlife Day Care and Elementary

Education in the afterlife isn't like the earthly kind. Children develop the importance of peace and love, and are given the opportunity to share that with their family here on earth, but as their soul continues to advance they may take on the role of a spirit guide to someone who they may not have known in their lifetime. It could be that Winnie may guide another child diagnosed with her same cancer. Helping that child as they go through treatments, and possibly helping that child as they journey to the other side. Or she might help guide someone who might've lost a parent and need to see that there is light in the darkness.

Rock-A-Bye

It was Lorna's first pregnancy and everyone commented on how wonderful she looked. She felt good too, and was confused by all the complaints and horror stories her friends shared of their pregnancies because she experienced none of that. Other than some minor nausea, she never had morning sickness, and barely had any heart burn. Everything seemed perfect. It wasn't until she felt the baby kick for the first time that it finally set in that she and her husband Spencer were going to be parents. She had first mom jitters, and although a confident career woman, she realized she was becoming a cautious mommy.

"That's normal," her sister Sara, told her. "You aren't neurotic; this is just all new to you."

Lorna tried her best to relax, but intuitively she didn't like that everything was almost too perfect, right down to measuring perfectly with her due date. She couldn't quite put her finger on it, and even her obstetrician laughed at her when she vocalized her trepidation.

"Lorna, the ultrasound is fine. Baby is kicking. Your bloodwork is great. You have six more weeks before you're up all night long for the rest of your life with worry," the doctor laughed. "Enjoy this peace. And if there's any indications from your pregnancy, this baby boy will be easy peasy."

Lorna laughed back in response. She knew that wouldn't be entirely true, but she loved her doctor for calming her fears.

That night Lorna awoke in a panic, and told Spencer she wanted to go to the emergency room.

"Really, Lor? Maybe just call Dr. Wagner instead," he suggested, hoping he could just roll back over and fall asleep. That didn't happen though, and he knew Lorna wasn't a cry wolf kind of a person.

So, both wearing pajamas, they walked into the emergency room without any real symptoms other than a feeling. Just a few hours later Lorna and Spencer were cradling their newborn in their arms. Everything was seemingly perfect, but just as Lorna began to feed Wyatt, he started turning blue and the room became a haze of medical professionals. Wyatt was rushed out of the room as Lorna and Spencer looked on in shock.

The next day Spencer wheeled a numb and grieving Lorna out of the hospital, empty handed. Wyatt passed away just two hours after delivery. Without explanation or insight, they returned home to an empty house and a full nursery with his brand-new stroller sitting near the door. They weren't ready to give him back to heaven. Their hearts felt shredded.

There was no warning, and even after an autopsy they were no further educated on the why of it all. It was the regret that Lorna held on to that made her begin to drown in depression, suicidal even. She had a feeling, she kept saying. She should've followed through and she didn't. Sobbing didn't purge the ache, nor did counseling.

At the three-month ultrasound they had learned the baby was a boy. Neither of them cared about the gender, they just wanted him to be healthy and to raise a happy child. Spencer loved westerns and couldn't wait to play cowboy with him, so they named him early on—Wyatt John.

The pending arrival of the baby brought showers and gifts from family and friends, and the nursery began to fill with necessities and an apparent love of a baby that many were anticipating. Wyatt's washed clothes sat neatly folded in the white washed dresser that Lorna lovingly created from a yard sale find, which Spencer made fun of her for. "It's not like I dumpster dove," she laughed, when he accused her of being silly and said they could just buy him a new dresser. "But I want him to know that we spent every thought on his arrival, not just money," she replied. That day was filled with laughter, she thought back, as she sat in the rocking chair holding on to a stuffed teddy bear that her dad had brought to the hospital when he found she was having the baby. She wished so badly it was her son she was hugging.

Spencer didn't know how to make it right, all the while knowing at the same time there would never be righting this karmic wrong. With his own heavy heart, he consumed the first week after with work and crying in private. When his mom noticed the soul ache, she reminded him that he could do something and that was to not avoid his wife, his grief, or his strength. But Lorna wanted nothing to do with him. She spent time in her own angry energy, pushing him away. "It will take some time," people sympathized. But that same heavy fog that she felt, he felt too. Even the joyful songs of the morning birds angered him.

It was a morning jog by himself when Spencer came upon a sign that he felt was from Wyatt. He'd jogged the path just about every day but was stopped when he saw a yellow finch that must've just passed.

"That's so sad," said another jogger noticing the passed bird. "There's an omen that a dead sparrow or finch is a sign from beyond," the stranger explained.

"Or maybe it simply died," Spencer shrugged his shoulders, and using a large piece of mulch moved the bird to the grassy area.

"Maybe," the stranger continued to comment ignoring Spencer's cynicism. "But I bet it's a child saying they're okay,"

Without another beat, she jogged away.

Spencer stood there staring at the small bird and looked up to heaven. "Could it be?" he wondered. Shaking his head in disgust at even spending an iota of time on spiritual nonsense, he turned back around toward home and was surprisingly greeted by Lorna.

"Spence, I heard a child's laughter," she clapped her hands together and smiled the first smile he'd seen in a while. "I think it's Wyatt telling me he's okay."

Hesitating for a moment, he decided to not share his dead bird encounter, although finding it ironic they both had, what the stranger testified as a heaven hello, the same day, around the same time.

"It's got to be Wyatt telling us he's okay. He made it to the other side," Lorna sighed in relief as she re-told her encounter again.

Spencer had no doubt that Wyatt went to heaven and he was confused why Lorna was holding on to the wondering when she answered without being probed.

"Our moms and dads are all here, and we are lucky to have our grandparents too. I've wondered who is taking care of Wyatt, if anyone is. He's just a tiny soul."

Spencer wasn't raised religious, but he did believe in heaven and hell, and never thought of a baby having to be taken care of as a worry. The next morning as he went to leave for work, on the doorstep there was another dead yellow finch.

"It's got to be an omen," he told his friend and coworker.

"Did you—?"

"I can't tell Lorna," he interrupted before his friend finished. "She'd think we were cursed, I'm afraid. To be honest, I kind of feel like maybe we are," he confessed soberly.

"My mom and grandma are into omens and legends, and that's not what I remember the meaning of a finch being."

"Maybe a live finch, but Jeff, this feels different. They were dead."

"No, I'm talking about a dead finch. Here let's look," Jeff opened his laptop to an internet browser and put in the key words "dead finch meaning" and, sure enough, site after site described how it was a sign from heaven.

Small birds, such as finches and sparrows were sent into mines to see if there was enough oxygen level. If they came back, it was fine. If not, it was potentially toxic and the miners would find an alternative route. They were their protectors. They sacrificed their lives to save another's life.

"Maybe there's something more than what it seems. If you don't believe me, though, maybe you need to see her," Jeff dropped a business card on Spencer's desk, closed his laptop and walked back to his cubicle. The business card read: "Kristy Robinett, an Abnormally Normal Psychic Medium."

———

I was sitting at a table in the lobby of a library, signing books, when I saw a couple staring at me, as if they wanted to ask something but were afraid to. Chuck, my husband, was sitting next to me, and motioned for them to come over.

"Don't be shy," Chuck gestured. "She won't bite, but I might," he joked, got up and made an excuse to step away. He was picking up on their apprehension as well.

"I know you aren't giving readings, and we're staying for your lecture later on, but..." the lady apologized, holding the hand of what I assumed was her husband. With her other hand, she nervously pulled her hair in back of her ear.

Standing next to the couple was the spirit of a small boy, about two years old. He held the hand of an older gentleman who was wearing a red and gray flannel shirt and blue jean overalls.

"Your little boy is fine. He's in heaven and with your..." I pointed to her husband, "... grandpa."

They both looked at one another in surprise and for a moment I thought maybe I made a mistake. Maybe she hadn't lost the baby yet and it was a future happening. Or maybe I shouldn't have said anything at all, but the man leaned forward and whispered, "Is my son showing you anything?"

It was a question that makes me cringe so much that I call it the Houdini question.

Harry Houdini, the famed magician from the 1920s, was very close to his mother. His mother believed in the spiritualist movement, but Harry, being a magician and knowing that the eyes can see something that is manipulated, was a huge skeptic. When his mother died, he sorely wanted to contact his mother and he began to contact mediums and others in the world of the supernatural, but witnessed fraud after fraud. Feeling dejected and mad, he focused on calling out the frauds and fakes. Interestingly enough, he had several friends who were spiritualists and who did believe in communication from the afterlife and to prove to them that he had an open mind, just a grieving heart and a dislike for deceit, he, with his wife Bess, set up a code word for when either of them journeyed to the beyond.

Houdini spent most of his career after his mother's passing focused on exposing what he called "vultures who prey on the bereaved." Houdini joined a panel that was put together by *Scientific American* magazine, which offered a reward for any medium that could prove their psychic gifts were genuine. In every city along his tour, Houdini offered $10,000 to anyone who could prove their so-called gift. The shows sold out all over the country, but not without some strange mishaps. "Maybe you shouldn't be mocking the supernatural," some of his friends warned. During that tour, on Halloween in Detroit, Houdini was punched in the abdomen. His appendix ruptured and despite lifesaving measures, he died. Bess Houdini immediately put out the word that she would offer the $10,000 to anyone who could offer their special code word from the afterlife. In 1928, a man named Arthur Ford contacted Bess to say he had a message from Houdini. Bess reviewed the message and it was in fact their code word—BELIEVE.

Unfortunately the *snap your fingers* and produce the sign, the word, a birthdate, etc., isn't always possible in that moment. The little boy, however, handed a yellow finch to me. Whether it was what they were looking for or not, I decided to share the message. "He wants to hand you a yellow finch as his message telling you that he's okay."

He gasped and turned toward his wife. "I need to tell you something," he confessed.

"You keep hearing Wyatt. Well, after his passing I kept finding dead finches and thought it might be a sign that we were cursed." He stopped and looked at me, "Is that what it means?"

The older gentleman shook his head in disagreement. "Tell that beautiful couple I'm caring for their son, and he is fine. They had to sacrifice him so that *she* could live."

It's not up to me to connect the dots, but to get as many dots as I can from heaven and offer the dots that will hopefully eventually connect. I asked the elderly spirit to tell me more, if he could.

Be Mine

The older gentleman's name was Weber Bryans, and he was born in 1900 on a farm in rural Iowa. His dad, a typical farmer, was a hard worker, but his husband and father skills were more than lacking.

"My father believed that kids should be beaten into discipline," Weber told me.

The more you coddled, the more they acted up was his parenting. A Gospel reading at night, along with a whipping after dinner to keep him and his fourteen siblings godly was the norm. When Weber was just fifteen years old he decided he couldn't do it anymore and he asked his brother and sister, twins, and just a year younger than him, if they wanted to escape the farm with him. No, he wasn't sure where he was going, but he decided that anywhere was better than the hell he and his siblings were living with. As much as his brother and sister wanted to go, they were afraid that they would be caught because they'd slow him down and the repercussions would be far worse than what they were going through now. Weber was sad, but he understood. "If I can, I'll come back and get you," he promised, that night underneath the full moon. He winced at his whip marks as he turned over in the twin sized bed that held two more of his brothers.

The next morning, May 15, 1915, he did his chores, kissed his mom on the cheek, and then went off to school, only he had set his watch for when the train stopped at the depot. Instead of school he was hopping on the train to wherever. Without any fear or guilt in his heart, he jumped on an empty rail car, took out the blanket from his worn bag and sat on it. Dusk was about to set when it stopped again. His stomach hungry, and his heady woozy from the vibration of the tracks, he stood on his wobbly legs and jumped off.

Fate would land him in a small town in Tennessee where most families were made up of miners. For a week he hid in a barn that looked to be cared for by a small family. He stole leftovers, pet their Bassett Hound, who never barked even once at him. More than likely because he shared his food, he reasoned, and listened to the family happily sing hymns after dinner. Then he was discovered.

Instead of shipping Weber back, they listened to his story and made room for him in the barn with his own cot. There were chores he was to do, school work that he had to keep up with, and responsibilities he had to complete. Weber wasn't a bad person like his father tried to make him believe. He was respectful and a hard worker. He taught the littlest girls how to read, and the man of the house showed him woodworking. It was different for him to be accepted and it took a long time for him to feel comfortable.

Even before Weber graduated from high school, he began to work in the mines. It was low pay, long hours, and awful conditions, but each night he would come back to a loving family and that was worth it for him at the end of the day. He told his new family he never knew that birds sang, or noticed the seasons as much as he did now. He was no longer hiding.

Just after graduation he met the woman he called Sweeties, and they married in a small spring wedding atop the mountain underneath a large elm tree, to the whip-poor-will's song. He had sent notice to his siblings where he was, and asked them to join him. His mail was ignored, or so he thought. Weber was used to disappointment, but nothing was going to stop his happiness.

Several months after the wedding he found out it wasn't that his family didn't want to respond, they couldn't. A worn black and white news clipping explained:

May 15, 1915

   Fire was reported at the Bryans homestead just before midnight. Despite several stations from two counties, all lives were lost.

It took Weber awhile to realize his family had died the same evening he disappeared. Did they even know he was gone? Did the community believe he perished in the fire too? Did his father start the fire because he was gone? Or was it a tragic accident and his life was divinely spared? It was questions that would haunt him until he took his very last breath, at the age of eighty-two years old. He had three children and six grandkids and was excited on his journey to meet up with his Sweeties who'd past a decade before. He never moved on from his grief, but he kept the love.

"You see," he told me, "My heaven is surrounded by the people I loved, not the people who I just wanted to love me. The wind is a soft breeze, the temperature is perfect, and I get to hear the whip-poor-will's song because it brings me back to my happiest time with Sweeties, who still wants to be with me and who loves me. Even into eternity," he laughed.

"Sacrifices are made every moment, but we are unaware of it at the time. We often forget that each breath, each minute we are alive, is because someone gave up something or someone for us. The fragility of that finch is a message to them that life is delicate, and that baby boy gave up his life so his sister could live. Through them they are to teach her that. She doesn't owe anyone, just as they don't owe anyone. It's not an owe," he explained, stuffing his hands into his pockets. "No, it's so much more than owe. It's hope. It's gratitude. It's forgiveness."

"So there'll be another baby?" the woman looked at me unconvincingly.

Baby souls are cared for in a sort of nursery where other spirits help love and assist them in their journey, whether it is to stay on the other side or incarnate into another lifetime. I could see Weber holding the soul of a baby and made a motion that it was already sent.

"There's one now. I believe you're pregnant now," I responded, taking a book from someone who'd been patiently waiting for me to finish and signed my name.

When I looked up they were gone.

I'm not certain if they even stayed for my lecture they said they were planning on attending, but nine months later I received a postcard in the mail. With a yellow finch colored border, a baby girl dressed in pink lay swaddled in feathers and a sign that read *Welcome Hope Weber Bryans*.

A note attached read that they believed Hope was heavenly sent from the miner they never knew, Spencer's great-grandfather, and baby boy Wyatt, who believed that Hope was needed. "We realized heaven doesn't punish, heaven heals. Heaven forgives, and heaven gave us Hope."

Chapter Two

Terminated Souls

No matter your belief in what's right, pro-life or pro-choice, it may be a human who decides the earthly fate of the soul, but it is not a human who decides the fate of the soul in the afterlife. Choices are never without emotional consequences. We so often are our own worst enemies, and in the situation of a miscarried, aborted, or terminated soul, the would haves, should haves, and could haves can be forever haunting.

Return to Sender

It didn't take a line on a pregnancy test to let her know that the results were positive. Between tender breasts, an extra tender heart, and a missed cycle, she knew weeks ago. Everything in between and after, though, was an uncertain. For a nineteen-year-old who thought she knew everything, it all came crashing down as she stared at a harmless line on the EPT.

Olivia had been with her boyfriend since senior year of high school. He wasn't her type according to her friends and family, but at her age how would she or anyone else even know what her type was. There was a connection that made her fall in love with him every time they were together. She joked that he had her under his spell, and he said the same of her.

When they graduated, they both decided to stay at home, go to college, and work. Most college days ended up being skipped, though, and they'd find themselves sitting in a park and talking. Paul was quick to promise her a beautiful future together, and Olivia drank every word with savage thirst.

Paul took almost all of her time, and with her friends away at school, she was left without anyone else to confide in. It didn't matter, she'd excuse, he was her best friend anyhow and he would always be there for her. Staring at the test, she knew she had to meet with him and they needed to discuss what was next. It looked like the promise of the future would have to be moved up to promises for today. So the next day, they skipped school and met at their spot, the top of a hill surrounded by weeping willows.

"Who did you fool around with?" Paul screamed, throwing the pregnancy test back at her.

"Only you," Olivia sniffled, wiping her quick tears. "You're my first and my last, Paul. How could you think otherwise?"

Paul stood up and turned his back. Hands clenched behind his head he let out a tribal scream. Olivia stood and wrapped her arms around him in comfort, but he pushed her hard away.

"You'll get rid of it," he warned. "I have some savings, and I guess I'll pay for it. Make the appointment." Without another word he stormed off toward his car leaving Olivia confused and stunned.

There wasn't anyone to confide in. She knew her parents would be disappointed and she couldn't bear their reaction, but they picked up on her agitated mood, asking her if she was okay, and if she fought with Paul. She decided to explain it as a lover's tiff, but the fear of what to do, or what not to do, was frightening, and Paul wasn't answering any of her calls. She realized that for the last couple years she'd been conned. She gave up her friends, a college scholarship, and now she was about to give up a baby too. It wasn't that she wanted to have an abortion, but she knew she couldn't take care of him or her either.

It was a cold spring Saturday morning when she drove to the clinic from home fifteen miles away to have the procedure done. She was met by several protestors outside with signs showing grotesque images and some with Bible verses pasted upon them.

"You're sealing your damnation," a lady told her, grabbing her coat sleeve. "And you're sending your baby's soul to hell. How does that make you feel?"

Unable to speak, she opened the clinic's door and walked through to a waiting room filled with women of all ages, all looking frightened and regretful. Many had someone with them, and although she was instructed she would probably need a driver too, she had nobody. The last conversation with Paul ended with him calling her some choice names, hanging up and blocking her number. She couldn't believe she actually looked for his car in the lot when she pulled up, hoping that he'd come to his senses, be by her side and tell her everything was okay. But his car wasn't there, and this wasn't a movie. As she filled out the paperwork, she stared at the empty space next to "Driver" and painfully added "None." She lied to them that she only lived a couple blocks away so they would let her leave without one.

After Olivia filled out her paperwork, she was called back for a so-called counseling session to make sure that she was ready. She wanted to laugh because who was ready to terminate their baby, but she played along and answered the questions the way she knew they'd want them answered. Yes, the father knew. It was true, Paul did. Yes, she was sure. Nope, she really wasn't, but didn't dare admit it. Yes, she was going to school and her future plan was to graduate and a child would not be convenient. No, she wasn't financially stable to take care of a child. She took pop cans back and withdrew her birthday money to pay for this. Ironic, that money from her birthday would help create a death date. She tried to push that thought out of her mind, though. Yes, she thought about adoption, but she was certain this was what she wanted to do. She signed three pieces of paper, handed a prescription for a pain killer to get filed afterward, and was sent back out into the waiting room until it was her time.

For two hours she watched a dozen girls walk in, and then walk out an hour later. Some were crying, some were doubled over, most looked numb. One of the girls had to be no more than thirteen as her mother held her hand and walked her out of the dark clinic. Each time the outside door opened, the protestor's chants filled the lobby.

"You're not just killing a baby, you're killing a soul."

"Your baby has a heartbeat."

Olivia tried to muffle out their demonstration. "They didn't know, she screamed in her head. They had no idea how hard this decision was for me, for anyone."

Her name was finally called. Well, not her given name, a pseudonym—Anne. Anne of Green Gables was one of her favorite books and when she chose it she felt like an orphan too.

The nurse handed her a gown and told her to change, put her incidentals into the locker and go to room number six, lay on the table, feet in the stirrups. Hand shaking, she did as instructed and slammed the locker door, taking the key and wrapping the yellow band around her wrist. It reminded her of her locker in gym class. Her least favorite class. Opening the door to room number six she tried not to look at anything, and just got up on the table and laid down. Pinned to the ceiling tiles were photos of clouds, as if that would make everything all better. The doctor and nurse came in and the procedure began. It hurt. It hurt a lot as she tried to stay strong and stifle her cries. She thought maybe if she cried it would muffle the noise of the machine that was taking her baby away. She wanted to jump up and tell them to stop, that she'd changed her mind, but the doctor patted her on the calf and told her she'd done great and she was all done. The nurse helped Olivia off the table and to a room where there were several girls lying on cots.

"Here's some Tylenol. Lay here for a half hour, and then we'll let you go home."

Again, she did as instructed, avoiding the looks from the other girls.

"Do you have cramps," the girl to her right asked her between Olivia's sobs.

Olivia nodded that she did, biting her bottom lip.

A young lady about eighteen years old called out across the room, "Girl, this is my seventh abortion, it only gets worse as the night goes on."

"Do you feel guilty?" the sobbing girl asked Olivia.

Again, Olivia nodded, and this time she couldn't stop the tears she had stuffed deep in her throat. She released.

———

It was twenty years later when Olivia sat across from me in my office. Her mother, who had passed away the year before, was there in spirit with a baby in her arms.

"I don't have kids and don't care to," Olivia said to me defensively when I told her what I saw.

"Your mom says it's a baby that you may have miscarried."

Olivia stared at me.

"Or terminated," I added.

A bank executive, Olivia was dressed well. Wearing a gray pant suit and shiny black heels, she was put together from the outside, but there were scars that had never healed on her soul.

"Mom says you need to forgive yourself, and she's not judging you. She never knew what you went through. She wished you'd confided in her, but she understands why you didn't."

Olivia continued staring at me for a long time before answering.

Her eyes narrowed. "Was it a boy or a girl, can you tell?"

My guides showed me pink, which was my sign for a girl. Olivia jerked her chin upwards when I answered and willed the tears to stop by pressing her fingers into her eyes, not minding that she was rubbing her eye makeup.

"I always thought it was a girl," Olivia whispered. "Is she mad at me? Did I cause her eternal damnation?"

With approximately half a million abortions legally performed every year, just in the United States, it was a question I received a lot and was always met with raw emotion.

I always see the soul of a termination or miscarriage still in baby form, while a child that was born, even if living just minutes, grows and typically shows themselves to me at the age they would've been on earth. No matter whether a child is lost through termination, miscarriage, or at birth, we still have a soul which has wisdom, intelligence, and love. For me, though, I don't have the communication that I would with an older soul. There is always a spokesperson for them. It might be a grandparent, but sometimes it's their spirit guide or an angel. No matter who it is, they are taken care of and not abandoned in heaven, and they aren't damned to an eternal hell either.

So often those who've had a termination or abortion experience self-persecution, imagining some sort of eternal punishment in the afterlife. Spirit understands the pain and guilt associated with the decision, and knows that throwing more anguish on the burden helps nothing. The soul of the baby continues on and the soul of the parent and that child will always be linked. If I see three children for a person and they tell me that there are only two, I'm almost positive that there'd been a miscarriage or a termination because these souls still have a belonging with the parents.

Just as on earth, we are given free will to choose to reincarnate and move on, or to wait and reunite with loved ones. Olivia's child decided to wait, for a bit anyhow.

"It's time to stop punishing yourself. It takes time to start loving yourself again, but you're worth it, Olivia. Your mom thinks so too."

Olivia bowed her head, the shame of the years bleeding from her energy pores.

"Set yourself free. You help yourself, but you also help your baby. She's bound by your pain as well, and as you release yourself from the chains, she can move forward too."

"If I wanted therapy …," Olivia folded her arms in defense.

"I'm not a licensed therapist, I'm a messenger between the worlds and heaven wants you to heal. Never forget how strong you are, how far you've come. Sometimes there's never an apology, and that's what I'm thinking you've believed you needed all these years. We all have choices in our life. Some we do right, some we do wrong, some we wish we could have a redo. You can do the right thing now, by releasing all those chains."

"Does she have a message?"

Olivia's grandmother, who passed away when Olivia was fourteen years old, told me that she met the baby on the other side as soon as she passed, and she was named Vera. In Russian it meant faith.

"Grandma came from Russia," Olivia said, stunned.

"Your family is all together, in their heaven. Their family being all together was their heaven, your mom says, and that includes your unborn child."

Olivia left with a lot to think about. Sometimes I never hear back from a client, but two years later I was happy to see Olivia's name on my schedule, and pleased to see a baby bump.

"At almost forty years old, I never thought I'd have a baby. I never thought I deserved a baby after the abortion. I didn't trust anyone after Paul's betrayal and I stopped loving myself after I felt I betrayed the baby. Do you know the gender?"

"It's a girl," I confirmed.

"We're naming her Yana. It means light." Olivia smiled, handing me the ultrasound photo. "Do you think Yana might be Vera, Kristy?"

It was a common question. Is grandma my daughter, or did my favorite dog become my new puppy? It's not always easily answered with a yes or a no.

Sometimes we are gifted people in our life through a pre-arranged contract, and so with miscarriage or termination, that same soul may indeed attempt to have another chance to be in your life. It's not always linear, though. It may be that your grandson was your aborted baby, and not your son. It may be a female in the one incarnation and a male in the next.

Then sometimes you incarnate by happenstance or by accident, without any pre-arranged contract. It's simply a subconscious intention sent from a soul into the universe. Loss through miscarriage or abortion may result in a future incarnation, but again, it isn't a guarantee. It could be that a contract is made to be with someone else. So even though a child may come back to a parent, either the mom or the dad, there's no hard and fast rule.

You are always welcome to invite that soul back into your life, though. And that's exactly what Olivia did once she forgave herself, and worked on her forgiveness of Paul's actions, without his apology. She came to realize that people will hurt you, and people won't say sorry.

There's a meme that tells you to throw a plate on the ground and then say you are sorry. The plate is still broken despite the apology. Although an apology or lack thereof helps to show the character of the person apologizing, no apology can reverse the damage done. Yet so often we hold on to that lack of response and allow it to damage us further. It's not up to anyone else to fix you; it's up to you to move forward without their fixing.

"When Vera passed away, I immediately became her caregiver," Olivia's grandmother told me. "It was a position I didn't take lightly. I knew Olivia wasn't in the place to be a mom yet, but I knew she would be one day and that this child would be her daughter once more. It was a special undertaking, but my job on earth was a pediatric nurse. I suppose my soul had to have that wisdom in order to do this heavenly job so that I could grace earth with a piece of heaven."

————

Yana was almost three years old and playing on the floor of her room when Olivia asked her how she got to be so smart.

"Your grandma helped me," she said, quickly moving back to playing with her dolls.

Olivia sat, stunned, carefully choosing what to say next. "You didn't know my grandma, Yan."

"I did. I met her up there," Yana pointed toward the ceiling. "She took care of me until you could take care of me."

Curious now, Olivia decided to ask more. "What was it like there?"

Yana set down her doll and gazed at Olivia with a knowing. "It was beautiful. My home had flowers that I could pick and Babu ..."

"What did you say?"

"Your grandma's name, Babu ... her hugs made me feel like you were there, mommy." Yana got up and skipped toward the living room, leaving Olivia to her thoughts.

Her grandma was called Babu, short for *babulya*, which means grandmother in Russian. She never thought she'd mentioned that to Yanna. Her grandma, her mother's mom, was strict, but loving, and all she could do was look up and thank whomever took care of her baby, and for offering grace and forgiveness and giving her back to her.

Reincarnation

My daughter was three years old when she sat on the living room floor watching her cartoons and playing a game when she looked up at me and innocently said, "Mommy, remember when you died in that fire and daddy saved me and my brother?"

I squinted in confusion at her, wondering if her father had watched a fiery movie the night before that her subconscious picked up on.

"Well, honey, I'm still here," I put my hand on her back, "That didn't happen."

"Oh it did, and he knows it too," she said defiantly and pointing to my belly.

I hadn't told anyone other than my then husband that I was pregnant, and it was much too early to even know the gender.

"I was mad at you for dying," she said, tearing up, as if reliving it right there. "I even got this," she said and lifted up her long blonde hair where she had a birthmark.

"That's an angel kiss," I teased, tickling her tummy. "I'm here now," I said, holding her in my arms. "I won't leave you," I promised.

I had a miscarriage soon before Micaela was born, and I did have a fear of fire. At just a couple years old, Micaela knew more than she should've for her age. It was as if she was telling her soul's story.

Familiarly Unfamiliar

Observations in reincarnation research detail that souls don't always come back within the same religion, nationality, ethnic affiliation, race and/or gender. Each lifetime can change and reformat according to the wisdom they are to learn, share, and teach. It's to expand the soul's wisdom.

Since Adrian was born she fought the stereotype of what a girl was to be. Dolls were replaced with toy guns, and skirts with blue jeans and t-shirts. When she was five years old she found her mom's scissors and gave herself a haircut, not to just see what would happen, but because she didn't like her long locks. The kids at school made fun of everything that made her who she felt she was. Her parents supported her through her tribulations, but didn't understand it. "I don't want to fit in," she rebelled. "I want them to accept me for who I am." Labels are an unfortunate thing in this world; if you don't quite fit within that certain category, many feel that you are a misfit, and that's what Adrian felt like. "Are you gay?" her mom asked her one time when she was fifteen years old. She didn't know how to answer. It wasn't a sexual thing, it was a soul thing.

Adrian was intelligent and caring. She loved animals and, on the weekends, would volunteer at the local animal shelter. "Animals don't care about my name, or who I am, or what classification I'm in. As long as their tummy is fed and their ears are pet they are happy. Why can't we humans be like that?" she asked her dad when he picked her up. Her dad didn't have an answer. Her hurt was painful to everyone in the family.

It was the eve of Adrian's sixteenth birthday when they heard the gunshot. Adrian had carefully planned her ending, having wrote notes to her mom, dad, sister, brother, and best friend. Each note had a similar message: nobody could've helped take the pain away. She'd done all she could to show others that different wasn't wrong—it was right—but she was frustrated and she felt tired. She was sorry, she wrote several times, but this was her only way. "Maybe my next lifetime will be easier," she wrote to her best friend. "Thank you for loving me in this lifetime, never judging, never mocking, and never giving up on me. I'm sorry I gave up on me."

———

It was a blustery November day. The sky was gray, threatening snow, but instead it drizzled sad rain. It was only eight o'clock and I just wanted to snuggle under the down comforter and go to sleep. I couldn't fight my heavy eyes anymore and, despite the clock, fell into the hypnotic gaze of sleep. When I woke up I could make out the lights on downstairs, which told me that my husband was either still up or had fallen asleep on the couch, and I was going with the latter.

Sitting in the chair near my bed was the spirit of a young lady. Her brown hair was shaved in a military style. She wore an Ohio University shirt and ripped blue jeans that were cut larger than her small frame needed. She immediately apologized, taking blame for waking me. "I think you're going to see my mom and dad tomorrow," she said, turning her face away from me.

"Is that a good or bad thing?" I asked, trying to remember my schedule to see if she was right. I was still trying to wake up, though, so nothing came to me.

"I'm worried they're mad at me. They taught me to be strong and not to let the opinions of others get to me. I heard them, I just didn't know how to do it," she covered her mouth with her hand.

"So you took your life?"

Adrian nodded. With a deep sigh, she bit her lower lip, wishing away the tears. "Yeah, I did. I let it all get to me and now I think they're disappointed."

"Are you happy now?" I asked her, rubbing out the sleep from my eyes.

"I will be when they are. I know that is ridiculous. I just don't want them to think that they would've known something was up. Or they could've prevented it."

"And they couldn't have?" I inquired.

"Oscar worthy performance all my life," Adrian laughed. "A stellar one!"

I couldn't help but laugh with her.

"I was even ready to live a lifetime in hell to not live in this hell. What I found, though, is that we create our hell and we create our heaven here," she gestured upwards. "Or there," gesturing down. "Or here," she spread her arms out. "I could've done the work here and not caused all the pain that I caused" she said sharing her regret.

"So…?"

"Where am I? Well, it looks like I'm in your bedroom," Adrian joked and quickly turned serious. "After I shot myself, I didn't feel anything. It was like I was coated with Novocain from the dentist. Then I felt this light. I didn't see it, I felt it. Like mom wrapping me in a towel just out of the dryer. I could hear voices telling me to go back that it wasn't my time and voices telling me that they'd take care of me and that it was my choice—it was my decision. I didn't want to go back, though, even though I could see my family running into the bedroom and seeing me on the floor. Only, I wasn't on the floor. It was like I was seeing through a keyhole.

"I kept floating until I came to this older male energy who told me that he was my spirit guide and would help me, council me. I was angry. Where was he when I felt so alone? 'Right by your side?' he told me. 'Just like now.'

"I was taken into a room that was surrounded by windows wall-to-floor, and outside each window I could see my life experiences being played out. The day Mom and Dad had me, and their joy and excitement. The day I shot myself, and their pain. I could see in-between experiences too, like when I hit a home run during the softball tournament in middle school. And when we saw a rainbow on our camping trip. The time my best friend fell off her bike and I consoled her. Some experiences were happy, some were painful, but I was told that they were all the same—the experience. They helped me become who I was. It wasn't this," she pulled at her short hair. "It wasn't my eye color, or my gender, or about how many times I went to church. It was so much simpler than what we try and make it be."

She stopped to make sure I was listening. "Then I was asked what I wanted to do next. I was confused. Could I go home and make my wrongs, right? No, they meant did I want to live in my own hell or did I want to live in my own heaven. What feeling did I want to keep with me? It's not as easy of a choice as you might think," she said, now getting up off the chair. "I wanted to punish myself, and maybe I still am in a way because they are punishing themselves."

Adrian disappeared before I could ask her anything else. I had so many questions that I wanted to be Barbara Walters and do an interview of sorts. It took me awhile to fall back to sleep, but the next morning I was excited to see who was on my schedule. Sure enough, there was three one-person sessions and my last session was a two-person; it had to be Adrian's parents, and I couldn't wait to share their daughter's visit with me.

————

Clarence and Rhonda sat on the couch across from me and held hands as I shared my interaction with Adrian from the night before. Adrian's spirit did in fact show up, but she was much more guarded.

"She was guarded as a child," Clarence shared. "We'd try and hug her and she would pull away. Or if we asked her about school she'd be defensive and only give us the bare bones minimum, typically telling us what she thought would suffice. She wasn't manipulative at all. She was smart in some ways, but in other ways she was like a child that still needed to grow and she refused to. She was angry with the world, with us, for not making her normal."

"She now understands that there isn't a normal."

"You said she's got short hair and kind of dressed grungy," Rhonda began. "That's how she lived here. How …?"

I smiled. "We don't have physical bodies on the other side. We don't need haircuts or blue jeans. We don't need shoes or the necklace that her grandma gave her on her twelfth birthday. These things are what made up who she is. If she were to walk in the door in the physical it would be what you would recognize her with, right?"

They both nodded.

"If I were to say she had on a dress and long hair braided and tied back with a ribbon you would doubt that it was your daughter I was talking about."

"That makes a lot of sense. I saw her in a dream and she was dressed just like you said. It was the last thing she was wearing and I thought I made that up in my mind. Is that her only outfit," Rhonda asked. "Like do I need to be really careful with what I wear because I'll be stuck in eternity with horrible clothes?"

We all laughed, Adrian included.

"In all seriousness, though, I just want to know one thing—is she happy, Kristy? She lived her short life, all her life, unhappy. I just want her happy."

Adrian turned around, as if to disappear again and I stopped her. It seemed to be her built in personality to bail when things got tough. She did it in life, she did it in death, and she was doing it in the afterlife. "This is not helping you learn," I told her. "You face your fears head-on in order to release them."

"I'll be happy when they stop blaming themselves," Adrian said, looking down. "I can move on when they can."

She was asking almost the impossible and it was a hard message to even share, but I did. "As you work on you, she works on herself. It's a team effort. She's not unhappy, and you can't make her happy there anymore than you can here. Give her time. Let her learn and grow, but just know you did everything you could for her."

Unfinished business with someone who passes unexpectedly or from suicide is often debilitating for the survivors. Feelings of guilt and all the things that "could have," "should have," or "would have" been said dance around your imagination and damage the healing of closure and forgiveness. The "if only" is never a good course of action. You can't beat yourself up over things that were left unsaid or things that you would have done differently.

Adrian was an old soul, filled with a lot of wisdom, but just because you are wise doesn't mean that you can't grow.

Speak Up

Eight pounds, eleven ounces, and twenty inches long, the nurses handed my newborn son Connor over to me in the recovery room. I had another cesarean and the pain medication was making me fall asleep, only to be jolted awake with him in my arms, making me worried that I would drop him. But his even temper and quiet demeanor shined from that first moment on. He wasn't even an hour old when Connor's father told me that our baby boy had a cleft palate. I didn't have a clue what that meant or what it entailed, all I knew was that he had ten fingers and ten toes and was beautiful. It was when they handed me a bottle to feed him that I realized that something was wrong. They told me that they were going to have to transfer him to Children's Hospital, without me in tow, but I said, "over my dead body," so they brought the staff of Children's Hospital to me and showed me that I would have to feed him with a squeezable bottle, squeezing to his sucks. The next day a doctor informed me that Connor would never sing, whistle, or suck out of a straw, even after his surgery. His cleft was like a straw with a hole in it.

———

"How's March 17th?" the surgeon asked. Connor was almost a year old and it was time to repair his cleft. He'd already had various other ear surgeries, but this was the big one, and I was a mess. "Saint Patrick's Day—I'd call that a lucky day," he added, pointing to his own red hair and his shamrock pin on his white coat.

It was one of the worst days of my life, having to hand him over to medical staff to complete a surgery that would take several hours. The next several months he couldn't bend his arms, for fear he would tear the stitches by putting his fingers or toys inside his mouth. He adapted and even learned how to walk with balance and grace.

"Why him?" I asked his pediatrician during one of his appointments. We had gone through genetic testing, which was fruitless. I had lost Connor's twin in utero and it was thought perhaps the blood flow stopped and Connor was the miracle, but even that couldn't be proven.

"I believe this boy here," the doctor said, patting Connor on the head lovingly, "has an old soul and old souls carry old wounds. Perhaps he spoke up for something and was marked. Perhaps he is supposed to learn to speak up for something today."

His pediatrician came from an old country that had old wives' tales, so I didn't take it particularly serious. I actually blamed myself for Connor's health issues, despite it not having anything to do with me, or his father, or anyone really. It was a fluke, I tried to remind myself.

Our Irish surgeon said that March 17th would be lucky for Connor, and with his Irish name, I do say that they were right. There is a quote that says life is ten percent what happens to you and ninety percent how you respond to it. Connor always shrugged it off and pushed forward. There's lessons to be learned by that.

During Connor's eighth grade valedictorian speech he told the crowd that he hoped to be an elected official one day, to serve and to protect the public. It made me smile. He was the helper as a child. A militant-like cleaner, at the age of two he would clean and arrange the house. He didn't want an overfilled closet, minimalist was good for him. Too much of anything simply complicated his life balance. It was rare to see him with kids his age, instead he'd rather sit and talk to a senior citizen, helping them, and listening to their stories.

"Smile," people still tell him. It isn't that he doesn't want to smile, it's just that it has to be worth it for him to smile. The cleft birth defect may very well be a reminder of that.

He was a fighter in a previous life, I'm sure. He was a fighter as a baby, and today, a criminal justice major, he's made it his mission to fight for others.

If you have a birth defect or birth scar, wear it proudly. It shows that you, too, are a fighter.

Chapter Three

The Ache of the Past

Old or wise souls often feel removed from the world of today, having a deep yearning for a home—not quite a physical place—that might sync them to a simpler life. The echo of a lifetime before still sits within the soul and subconscious without reminder of time, but holding on to knowledge and wisdom.

Since I was a little girl I knew I belonged in a place surrounded by lilac trees and lavender fields with a front porch with rocking chairs to sit and relax. I would mourn a place, but I had no idea where it was. It was not quite a city or location; it was more of a feeling.

Instead of the country, I grew up on a street in Detroit. It offered me one thing that I loved, though: lilac bushes. When spring brought white, purple, and pink lilacs bursting through, scenting the air with their sweet fragrance. To this day lilacs are still a favorite of mine, and often a reminder of my mom, now passed away.

We moved into our new home the last weekend of September 2016. With an acre of our own, and thousands of acres behind us, one of our favorite things became the discovery of new blooms.

On Easter morning a small magnolia tree showed off its pink flowers, hidden behind a pine tree. We hadn't even noticed it before. And as April showers brought May flowers, the lilacs began to posture, and the hint of lilacs wafted around the yard with heaven scents of yesteryear and promises of what's ahead.

It's no wonder that in Victorian times widows often wore lilacs as a reminder of their lost love. And although all shades of lilac are beautiful, it is the dark purple shade that reflect spirituality and hints that the wearer is privy to the mysteries. Lilacs only bloom for about two weeks, which suggests that all beautiful things must come to an end, whether love or life. They remind us, though, that there will always be renewal if you can stay patient. Instead of mourning, keep the memory, and create new ones.

Ever since I was a little girl I dreamed of living in a farmhouse. The vision never really changed—a gravel road, lots of trees, the smell of lilacs in the spring, and peacefulness.

The architecture of the home wasn't important in my vision; a Victorian or a Cape Cod, it didn't really matter as long as there was a front porch. I kept the vision going by writing stories and poems and creating continuous vision boards. I pasted photos on the refrigerator, made screenshots on my computers, created Pinterest boards, and even changed my passwords to a variance of Ihavemydream-farmhome. There were days I felt defeated because it wasn't coming soon enough (in my timing), but I never stopped believing (thanks to the band Journey!).

Our ranch was a happy home. When Chuck and I married, we bought the home to raise our kids. On a tree lined street with neighbors who waved, annual block parties, and surrounding parks, great schools, and close to the freeway, I painstakingly landscaped the front and back with gardens and flowering trees. It had metal awnings that soothed our spirits on rainy nights and on autumn nights we could hear the distant roar of the local football games. That small home gave us a lot of memories of school dances, proms, graduations, weddings, holiday memories, book releases, and fun Halloweens. Our kids grown and in college, it was time to hand over the keys for new chapters.

It was the summer of 2016 when I decided on a whim to contact a bank to see about getting approved for a mortgage. Being self-employed made things a tad bit complicated, but to my surprise I was approved, and before my family could blink our small ranch home had a for sale sign in the yard and we were on a whirlwind search to find the home in my vision.

It was just a couple weeks after the home was listed that we began to receive bids, but our house hunt was idle and I began to panic that we'd be homeless if we accepted a bid, and I wondered if I was chasing a ghost of my own and that it didn't really exist. I knew every home for sale in the Michigan area. Every single one. Then I received an email from a stranger who was following me on social media that simply said my dream home wasn't here, it was in heaven, and to give up looking and take my house off the market. I thought she might be right. "Just be grateful for what you have," she sassed. It made me wonder for a brief moment. It had nothing to do with not being grateful for what I had, and here I was in my office, on the radio, and in my seminars talking non-stop about never giving up on your dream, and yet I felt like maybe the emailer was on to something.

"I need a sign as to what to do," I said out loud with a heavy sigh, throwing my head back and looking toward the ceiling.

Instead of festering, though, I had to go to the office and just leave it be for that moment. That's the funny thing about letting life organically work out; it often clears the way for magic and miracles to occur.

Believing Isn't Seeing, It's Being Open

I only had one appointment that day at my office, but it was a two-hour session with a large family. I pulled out some folding chairs to accommodate, lit some candles, and put on some piano music to help me meditate and allow my own earthly worries to fade.

Right on time, the family came and briefly fought over who would have what chair, and I began my spiel.

"Remember that the messages and those who come through might not be the messages and people you want, but what you need. Remember, I'm just the messenger and if you are really angry, there are some pillows there and you can throw them at me. I can take it," I teased trying to help them with their nerves and anxiety. Thankfully they laughed.

I'm always nervous that who my clients want to show up won't show up, but thankfully that has never happened. They might not be the first to show up, but they show up. I've also had many spirits who aren't quite invited show up too. This session, though, Meredith came.

Graduation had been the week before, and a group of friends decided to get together at the local lake.

"No drinking, right?" Meredith's mom asked, knowing all too well what eighteen-year-old kids did at the lake.

"Not for me, Mom, you know that," she reassured her.

It was true, Meredith was a good kid. She worked hard, got good grades, and was so excited when she got into her college of choice, the same college that her boyfriend Bobby got in as well. They liked Bobby too, and they trusted him as if he were their own son.

"Alright, well if both of you decide to do something stupid, just call me and I'll pick you up. Promise?"

"Yes, Mom, but that won't happen."

"And no Oregon."

When Meredith wanted to stay out late, her mom would text for her to not get pregnant. Somehow it autocorrected pregnant to Oregon and it became their inside joke. Meredith laughed and she gave her mom a hug and kiss on the cheek and ran out the door.

Bobby lived just a few miles away, but she had the newer car so she told him she'd just pick him up with her car and he could drive it.

They drove twenty miles outside the town and turned into the parking lot. After getting their belongings, they walked hand in hand through the dense wooded pathway that led to the lake and picnic area where they were going to meet their friends. It was just before noon but already bustling with people. The bright sunshine and warm June temperature made it the perfect day at the beach, and all Meredith wanted to do was lie on the beach towel and relax. Senior year hadn't been so easy for her. She had worked hard because she knew her parents worked hard and she wanted a scholarship to ease the finances. She did it, and for the first time in months she was able to lie down and take a breather.

Bobby was not a lie down and do nothing kind of a guy, though, and he wanted to hop on their friend's boat and go tubing.

"Look, you can lie in the boat and tan and I'll tube. It's a compromise."

"Or I lie here and you go in the boat. I like that compromise even better," she laughed. Putting her lips up to his, she playfully hesitated momentarily and nibbled his bottom lip.

"Ouch!" he said joking.

She knew, though, he wouldn't let up, and she couldn't resist his baby blue eyes. "Fine, let's go." She picked up her beach towel and threw it in the bag. Wrapping her arms around his tanned shoulders she gave him a true kiss. Grabbing her hand, Bobby led her to the boat and helped her on. "This'll be fun," he grinned.

She knew that she wouldn't be able to just lie in the boat. She'd been this route before too. Instead she was the official spotter for the six friends that had jumped in for the run.

"Your turn, Merrie," Bobby called.

"No," she resisted. She loved the water, but never felt safe in the water. "I'm good here."

"I'll go with you. C'mon, you need to cool off."

Again, Bobby wasn't taking a no, so she reluctantly peeled off her white shorts and put on a life jacket. Bobby helped her climb in and they sat beside one another. "Not too fast, okay?" she yelled out to her friend Zac who was driving. He nodded, but she wasn't convinced he wouldn't go crazy.

After a couple slower runs around the lake, she was feeling more comfortable and enjoying herself. She gave the thumbs up to go faster, and Zac happily obliged.

———

The news report that night read:

A beautiful summer afternoon came to a horrifying end for several teens celebrating their high school graduation when

Meredith Hopkins died after being run over by a speed boat while tubing with her boyfriend Robert (Bobby) Mazart.

Meredith fell off the tube and as the boat circled around she was run over by another boat, with injuries to her torso and head. She could not be revived and passed on the scene.

The first 911 call was made just before three o'clock p.m., with dozens of others trying to assist and calling for help. Emergency personnel rushed to the scene within five minutes as Meredith's friends assisted her back to shore.

———

Meredith stood between Bobby and her mother, who sat in front of me.

"He couldn't save me," she sighed in contemplation as I shared the message.

"Yes, I could have," he said punching his right leg. "I should have never pressured her to go on that tube. I should have let her tan like she wanted to."

Meredith's mom put her hand on Bobby's shoulder. "You know as well as I do that Merrie never did anything she didn't want to do if she really didn't want to do it. Remember the time …"

Meredith interrupted with a laugh. "I love the 'remember the time' they play. It reassures me that my memory won't be lost."

Bobby put his head back and rubbed his forehead. "I've never heard a blood-curdling scream like she screamed. It will haunt me forever."

Meredith looked worried. "I want him to be okay. I want him to go on to college, and find a love, and get married, and have kids.

And I want to pick out his kids." Meredith began to tear up, but she was strong on earth and in heaven she was the same.

"Those on the other side sometimes don't understand the deep grief we have," I shared. "They live when we live. They move on when we move on. They don't forget and they don't want you to forget."

"They don't miss us?" Meredith's sister asked sadly, leaning forward.

"They do, but it's different than our missing. It's not hurtful, it's more nostalgic mostly filled with good memories."

"Does she remember the accident?" Bobby wondered, continuing to rub his temples as if trying to erase that day's memory and the emotional aftermath.

Meredith shook her head in answer. "I remember having fun and then I remember calling out for Bobby. Everything went black and when I woke up I was standing next to my body as it was being lifted into the ambulance. I saw my mom on the beach and wondered why mom came, and thinking something really horrible was happening. Frank ran into my mom's arms and they were both crying and carrying on. I realized they were upset about me. Before I could try and reach out to them my dog from third grade, Zippy, was at my side and then my Pop Pop who had passed during my freshman year in high school. And then there was my dad's mom who had died when he was only eight years old. I recognized her from photos. And one by one people from my past began appearing. As they got clearer, the ones alive in this world and lifetime grew dimmer, and I was in front of a bright light. The brightest light I've ever seen was before me and I felt like I was flying. My fears, sadness, anger, anxiety, and anything negative was erased, baptized away. I looked around and was surrounded by strawberry fields, and I knelt down and tasted the sweetest strawberry ever."

"Meredith was highly allergic to strawberries. Summer reminded her of that more than any time," her mom smiled.

"I was given a job to do, but first I must heal like their hearts have to. They will see me again, I promise them that, as long as nobody builds up a wall that prevents me from getting in."

"How do we know if we are building that wall?" Bobby asked.

I looked long at him without saying anything.

"I've been building a wall, haven't I?" he lowered his head.

"It can be destroyed, Bobby, and that takes time too," I explained.

"Tell my family I love them, and Bobby that I'm so happy we had the time we did. I'll be by his side whenever I can."

Meredith stepped away, trying to gain her energy, but it was too soon. It had only been six months and it was too soon. I was grateful that she got through with as much as she had.

"I want to believe," Bobby told me as we said our goodbyes. "How do I do that, Kristy?"

There are those who simply believe and those who need proof. So often those who needed the proof felt that heaven was a far-off place, beyond the pearly gates. But there's no true beginning or end, the body simply carries the soul until it needs to transfer, not the other way around.

"You know how you go to school with someone for years? You sit next to them through classes, but never really talk or know what's going in their life? You see them, you hear them, you can touch them, but you realize after all those years that you barely even know them?"

"Yeah, I guess," he replied.

"And then there's someone you just met and you feel like you've known them forever. They are more real and true to you than someone you might've known for ages."

"That's how it was with Merrie and me. The moment we met I felt like it would be forever with her."

"There's a difference between real and physical. Believing doesn't require seeing, it requires you being open and ready to receive your messages. The signs are there for those who want them to be."

"I think I want to believe. I want to feel her around. I want her to forgive me."

"I don't believe she feels any forgiveness is needed. Try this, Bobby, on a clear night, sit outside and look up into the sky. If you feel something, the walls are coming down or have come down. If you don't, there's still work to do." I reached over and squeezed his shoulder. "It sucks, I know. I'm so sorry."

Bobby left with this head down. I took a few minutes to collect myself and decided to sit and meditate for a bit before heading home. After close to an hour, I was still feeling glum, but wanted to go hug my own kids, and that's when I heard a knock on my door. There stood Bobby.

"I went to the park down the road, trying to hear Meredith. I felt this urge to pick these lilacs and give them to you. I hope that's not creepy."

And there was my sign from an unexpecting teenager who'd lost his love.

"You heard heaven for sure, Bobby. Thank you."

Most days I wished I had a magic wand to make it all better. That day was one of them. Heaven is close by, but sometimes feels so far away. And sometimes it's the quiet whisper to pick lilacs.

Chapter Four

On Heaven's Timeline

Heaven doesn't always work on the timeline you want, rather the timeline you need, but as I grabbed my purse to go home my phone dinged through a message with a new house on the market.

"Look," I excitedly showed my husband when I got home. "It's got a wraparound porch, a pole barn, space for Dad, and…"

"And it's out of our budget," Chuck pointed out.

"But rumor is that the homeowners moved out of state and need the house gone, so they may take a lower bid if it works."

"And it's not the location we want," he continued, but noticing my energy wavering he relented. "See if the realtor can meet us there tomorrow."

"I'd hate for her or us to make that drive to just see one house, so I'll see if I can find a couple more to look at."

Honestly, we were tired. We were tired of cleaning the house. We were tired of dragging our animals out of the house for each showing, and we were tired of house hunting. It looked like so much fun on television, but the harsh reality was that it was too much like a blind date. The picture looked great on screen, but in the end it had all been one big catfish; deceitful photos and information to make it look better than it really was.

The next morning we were on our way to see what I was determined was our dream home. My dad was also burned out and decided to not go with us. "Let me know if you find something, Kristy. I'll stay here," he sighed.

As we pulled into the long driveway my phone rang. I was well known by my friends and family for not answering my phone, but I thought it was the realtor so I glanced and saw instead it was a friend and morning radio jockey. For several years I had been doing a bi-weekly segment for his morning show, but my visit the week beforehand felt off. I hadn't mentioned it to anyone, including Chuck, but when I saw his name on my caller ID I knew.

"Hey Kristy. Hope you're doing great," my friend chatted.

"Yeah, I am. I think I'm sitting outside what is my dream home," I shared, trying to make small talk but the butterflies in my stomach were floating into my throat.

"That's great. I hope it works out for ya." I heard him take a deep breath before continuing. "Well, I'm sure you saw this coming, but the show is making some changes and, well, your segment just isn't working anymore."

I could tell by his voice that his boss had given him the dirty work, and he did sound sympathetic.

I did know it was coming, but it didn't make it any easier. I tried to hide my disappointment and we ended the call that lasted less than a minute in length. I wasn't able to fill Chuck in before our realtor pulled up. Wiping my tears back, I got out of the car to walk into my new house.

Except it was a disaster. Nothing about it was dreamy, as if the morning couldn't get any worse. We stood on the porch and overlooked the field when I told Chuck that my segment had been cancelled.

"Now, Kristy, how could you get fired on your day off?" Chuck joked, paraphrasing a quote from the movie *Friday*.

I tried to laugh by adding, "Not just getting fired on my day off, but getting fired from a job that I don't get paid for!" It was true. My radio segments were just PR, not income. The tears fell before I could end the sentence, which I knew was just stupid.

The realtor locked up the house and walked over as I again wiped away my tears. "One more, right?" she smiled.

I nodded, but was feeling defeated.

"Let's just take the house off the market if this doesn't work," I told Chuck as we drove through the wooded street to the next home. "I can't do this anymore."

He didn't answer, but instead pointed as we rounded the corner of the gravel road to see a sprawling white cape cod with a painted green front porch. "There's no sign, but this is the address."

"This can't be it. This is what I've always pictured," I squealed, grabbing Chuck by the arm.

"I know," he smiled at me.

But it was the right house and as our realtor opened the door Chuck ran into the house like a kid coming down the stairs on Christmas morning. I simply stood in the hallway with the realtor and began to cry. Again. This time happy tears. I hadn't even seen the whole house, but I knew. I was covered in goosebumps and I knew.

I snapped a bunch of photos with my cell phone and couldn't wait to share them with my dad. It was perfect. I just knew it.

"Oh, can we stop at that cute shop?" I asked Chuck on our way home.

I personally think Chuck was thrilled to stop if it meant not talking about houses.

The small gift shop was so jam-packed with treasures that I could barely see the lady sitting behind the counter.

She had to at least be ninety years old, but her bright hazel eyes sparkled, excited to have someone to talk to.

"Let me know if I can help you with anything," she said, knitting what looked like a blanket.

I thanked her while I slowly looked around, admiring the many baubles and sparkles.

"Did you hear about that girl and her horse?" I heard the elderly woman say from the front of the store. I assumed someone else had come in and she was talking to them, but as I made my way up front I was still the only one there.

"Excuse me?"

"Did you hear about that girl Nicole and her horse?"

I had heard about it. Nicole was a local equestrian who had won ribbons on a national level ever since she was a teenager. She lived in a mostly rural area and would religiously ride her horse down the road past her house and then back every single morning, and every single evening when she got off of work. A delivery driver discovered her horse wandering nearby and recognized it as Nicole's horse. He got out of his truck and took the horse by the reins, guiding him back to the home when he found her body next to the road right in front of her house. She had been shot just once in her head and was deceased.

"Do you know that I think I know who did it, but nobody will listen to me?" the lady nonchalantly told me briefly looking up from her knitting.

Odd, I thought, that she was opening up to me—a stranger, but I believe that we all have people placed in our path for a reason, so I took the bait.

"I'll listen," I said, knowing that Chuck was waiting in the car and wondering what was going on, but he was used to this sort of thing with me—strangers telling me their life story, in both the physical and spirit.

"She came to me, you know?"

"Like her ghost?" I asked, trying to sound amazed.

"Yep. She sure did. I was a teacher back in the day and although I never had Nicole personally I wonder if maybe she just knew I'd listen to her."

"That's probably what it was," I said leaning in, now curious.

"She said that although the police think it was random, or perhaps someone shooting had accidently hit her," the lady huffed as if anyone would believe that, "but she was being stalked."

"Stalked! Stalked by who?" I exclaimed.

"Down the road there's a house," the lady clucked her tongue. "Residents tried to stop it and there ya go, now this."

"What kind of house? A group home?" I pondered out loud. The lady was adorable, but she was barely finishing her sentences and I felt like I was playing Wheel of Fortune with fill in the blanks to make sense of it all.

"Sort of like that. Apparently alcoholics and drug addicts go there to dry out in the country air. As if." She began to channel her anger into her knitting and with a missed stitch she let out a loud curse word. "I'm so sorry," she apologized, setting down her yarn. "I just don't understand how it's so very clear and nobody will do anything. That poor girl and her family. I know …," her voice wandered off and she picked up her knitting as if the conversation never happened.

"You know what?" I was now wondering if perhaps she had dementia.

"Maybe *you* can call the police and talk to them," she suggested with a sweet smile.

She didn't know me from Jane Smith or what my profession was. I looked around for a second to make sure there wasn't a camera crew, instead I saw Chuck looking in the window of the door, impatiently.

"Here, hon, I'll check you out. Your groom is waiting and I've taken all your time." She handed me my bag of small trinkets I had found.

"Do you believe in karma?" she asked me staring deep in my eyes. "Do you believe karma is real?"

"I do. I don't believe karma happens on our time table," I answered.

She nodded as if we had made a secret pact.

"Last week there was a lady in here. She walked right in, took an angel statue that was up to her hip, looked at me and walked out."

"What?" I sneered in awe at the gull. "Did you do anything?"

"No, honey. She could've had a gun and she could've hurt someone," she contemplated. "But I think that there is karma. Maybe she needed an angel. But then I wouldn't want that karma that came from it."

We both laughed. Although the conversations were a bit dark, she had lightness to her and she kept calling me sweetie and honey and angel and it felt endearing, making me wonder that if my grandma, my mom's mom, was alive, if she would've called me the same. She passed when I was four, but I always envisioned her as being the sweet and loving grandma-type.

"I'll check into the case and let you know," I promised with a smile and turned around and out the door to Chuck's questions as to what had taken so long.

We set up to see the house the very next afternoon with my dad, but even before I could pull into the driveway the realtor called. My heart sunk, thinking that the house had already fallen through before it could officially fall through. I wasn't typically so glass half empty, but I felt like I was on a roller coaster at this point. The call instead was to let us know we had a solid offer on our home and we had a day to make a decision with what to do.

The day after, showing my dad the house, we made an offer, and accepted an offer, and the next couple months would still be filled with a trying time all the way to the eleventh hour and beyond. When the bank decides to give you the mortgage just an hour before signing the paperwork, and the moving company decides to bail the morning of moving, you can go through many different emotions, and at one point I was sure we'd be homeless. So when we finally moved, I could hear angels singing and every one of my loved ones on the other side frustrated that I didn't trust them.

Every time I passed by the gift shop, though, I felt a sense of guilt as I still hadn't checked with the police on the case. Once we were moved in, though, I made a point of making some calls. The information I offered was shrugged off just like the lady said it was when she offered it.

"We're pretty sure it was random, Ma'am, but thank you for the tip."

The day after my conversation with the detective I thought I best tell the lady the bad news.

"She had to be late eighties, if not early nineties," I told the sixty-something-year-old woman standing at the counter. "I spoke to her for a long time. What do you mean there's nobody like that here? She rang me up and took my money even!"

"Was this her?" the lady opened up her pictures on her iPhone and showed me the sweet knitter who'd helped me.

"Yes! That's exactly who it was."

The lady furled her eyebrows and looked at me oddly. "That's my mom. She passed away in early July. She loved coming in to the store and helping us out. So you were here in the summertime?"

No, no, it was just a few weeks back, I wanted to tell her, but I thought it was best to not continue. Instead I told her how her mom was lovely and I was sure she was still watching over everyone. I knew it was the truth.

The case remains unsolved, but hopefully heaven can continue to find a means and a way to help with a break through. Was the elderly lady on the other side? Was Nicole? Were either? It was a case of spirit helping spirit, heaven helping heaven.

Chapter Five

Believing

There will always be those who don't believe in something and then there are some people who don't want to believe in anything. We are a "seeing is believing" kind of society. "Prove it or it doesn't exist" kind of world. Proof is shown through mediums, information from those who've had near death experiences, and then there's the Bible. Humans, however, find fault with everything unless they, themselves, can touch it, see it, feel it, hear it, and experience it. There will always be disbelievers and skeptics who try to debunk because they don't want to be seen as naïve or gullible. Sometimes, though, there is no explanation, and that too has to be accepted.

Hocus Pocus Heaven

Marla kept her composure as she sat across from me, stiff and formal, but her soul told another story, as did the spirit standing next to her.

"I don't really believe in this ..." Marla said, waving her hands in the air in a hocus pocus fashion.

"That's okay," I smiled. "You don't need to believe for it to exist. It makes it easier for me, and for them, but it isn't necessary."

If I had a dollar for everybody who said that to me in a day, well, it would be a lot of money.

Her husband stood next to her in spirit, smirking. He was obviously irritated as he attempted his communication with me, but with her lack of openness and his frustration I knew this session wasn't going to come easy. He showed me that he'd passed quickly, in an accident, on the way to a work conference. And he showed me a train.

"Did he collect trains?" I asked, only for Marla to shake her head no. "Do you live by trains?" She again shook her head. And then he showed me what would hopefully make sense.

"Marla, he said he passed on a train. He passed from a train accident?" It sounded like a question, but I knew that was what he was trying to tell me. It wasn't a usual passing so it caught me by surprise. Marla just stared at me, so I stated it again. "He said he passed away on a train. He shows me the train slamming into something and he was gone. Quickly. Just like that."

Marla still just stared at me so I continued and prayed that I was on the right track (no pun, honest).

"He says that he wasn't sure when he'd be back from the trip. It was an important presentation and he thought maybe a couple days, but it could've been a week. You were mad at him for not knowing because your anniversary was that week and you didn't say goodbye to him. He said you said that you'd see him when you see him."

Marla's eyes grew wide as tears formed. She whispered, "He's really here?"

I nodded and pointed over to where he was standing in spirit.

"I'm not mad. I'm sad. I can't get through this, Kristy. I feel like it's my fault and there's a void. Such a deep void." She winced as if in physical pain. "I'm simply walking around in a state of numbness waiting for my time. Is it my time soon?" she asked, hopeful.

We are taught that death is final. It's the end. We grieve and we get over it eventually.

Bull.

Death is far from final. It's not the end, it's a new beginning—for everyone. And we don't ever get over it. We walk through it. And then we walk backward and through it again. And sometimes we stop in the middle until someone pulls us through. Hopefully there's someone there to pull us through. There's no time frame. Just as you have a unique fingerprint, your grief fingerprint is unique too. The corporate world gives us three days to "get over it" and mourn. Our heart and soul tells us it will be a lifetime until we see our loved one again. The hurt is real. The heartache is crushing. And grieving is one of the hardest things you will ever do.

Marla was still in the beginning stages of grief and although I could bring through the connection, I couldn't take the pain away. What I did do was open up her line of communication with her husband. She wanted more from me, but it wasn't up to me to give her all the answers. I did, though, help her with her signs for over a year, plus.

Marla now does see his signs and they've helped break her frown so she sometimes smiles. She believes now. Not in any hocus pocus, not in me, but that death isn't final.

Death is like stepping into a different dimension, and there are visiting hours; it's just not what we think of as here.

"No, you still have time here, Marla, but he'll be waiting. And he said you have to live in his heaven since he got there first," I joked.

"Honestly? He made bad decisions. Please tell me when I get there I get my heaven," she said, her forehead wrinkling.

I couldn't help but laugh. Her husband was a joker and he was amused at her wondering.

"He said his heaven is a cabin in the woods, yours would be a high rise in a fancy building."

She returned my laugh. "He's right. We can compromise when we get there?"

I nodded. "Something like that."

Not everyone will be convinced there is another side. Some will be skeptical and cynical, and that is okay. Sometimes the grief is numbing and that is the way they deal.

It isn't up to me or you to convince anyone otherwise. Sometimes they just need a kind word, a hug, or a positive thought or prayer.

Create Your Heaven

My to-do list was becoming larger than I could handle, and panic was beginning to set in. With three book projects due within a few weeks, I was starting to feel the heat and it didn't have anything to do with the weather. My head was filled with an incredible number of thoughts that I was having a hard time pushing aside.

An eighty-year-old gentleman named Crofton came in for a session. His energy was laid-back and pleasant as he sat down and took in my office.

"Not what I thought," he said to me looking around my office.

I sat down across from him. "Most say the same," I replied, smiling.

"It's cozy. I like it." He studied me briefly. "I like you too."

I blushed and began to explain to him how I did readings, but he interrupted me before I could finish my first sentence.

"I'm not quite sure why I'm here, Kristy. I know that my wife and family are with me in spirit. I feel them around me. I know that I'm going to die soon. I have prostate cancer that's spread over time." He stopped, pulled out a handkerchief, and wiped away a few tears. "I guess I just needed to talk to someone. And you, Missy, are the chosen one." Crofton explained to me how he loved history and had joined a local historical society. "It was something to do, after all," he grinned. "Someone mentioned you, and it peaked my interest, so I booked an appointment. You are booked so far out that I thought my funeral might happen before this appointment!"

His quick wit and laughter was contagious and we fell into easy conversation as if he were a family member I hadn't seen in forever. His wife, son, daughter, and grandson came through in spirit and the sarcasm continued to be thrown from his relatives on the other side and back to them. The hour went by in a flash and I had to get on to my next appointment. But before he left, he hugged me. Holding me at arm's length, with his bright sparkling eyes he said he wanted to share a message for me too. "Pass it along if you want," he joked.

"After we're dead—sorry, transitioned," he corrected himself remembering that I didn't like the term dead. "After we've transitioned, it seems people finally listen to what we said and value what we did."

I nodded in agreement. Sad, but very true.

"Kristy, all those to-do lists, well they will always be there, but your family won't. Make sure to spend as much time as you can with them, because even though you can talk to them, you know as much as I do, it just isn't the same."

Crofton transitioned to the other side a year after our first and last session, but he had stayed in touch throughout that year sending me "I'm still alive" emails every so often, making light of his pending death. I hadn't thought of him for a while until I started panicking over my deadlines. Crofton shows up to give me hidden gems of wisdom, as he called it.

Whether you vacation or just spend an hour walking in the local park, make sure to take time to collect your soul pieces and find your heaven, like cookie crumbs along the way. So often, through the chaos of life, they become misplaced.

Chapter Six

Together We'll Find Heaven

There've been several incidents where I've encountered spirits who came through with a person that either accidently killed them, who died within hours of one another, or strangers who died together. After September 11th happened it was often that during a reading I would bring through a loved one of a client, and someone they wouldn't know. It was perhaps a co-worker or someone they'd clinged to at the last moment, their souls departing the earthly world in unison.

Recently I had a couple who came to see me in my office. Their daughter Dion had died in a tragic car accident. Another girl going the opposite way must've been distracted and crossed the double yellow line, running head on with their daughter. They were both pronounced dead on the scene, once the officers sorted out the scene, putting each driver with their correct car. Upon contacting their parents it was discovered the girls had been best friends since elementary school.

I didn't know the details until after I brought through Dion. "I swear I was just driving. I promise I wasn't texting, drinking, or even looking down. All of a sudden I heard a crash and Betty and I were standing on the side of the road."

"Is Betty with her now? If she is, we want nothing to do with her," Kim, the mother, frowned.

Betty was standing there with Dion, her head bowed in regret. "Tell them I understand. It was a terrible and stupid mistake. My phone dropped and I bent down to pick it up, taking my eyes off the road for just a second."

"A second that has ruined so many lives," Dion's mom exclaimed after I shared the message.

Dion was quiet while she watched the interaction. Grabbing Betty's hand in hers she asked me to give them a message that they wouldn't understand now, but hopefully would in the future.

"If Dion can forgive, find her heaven, and help Betty in return, then you need to work on forgiving too. It's important, she says."

But Dion's mom bit her bottom lip and shook her head in protest. "I will never. I can't."

None of us could convince her any differently, but several years later she came in for another visit holding a baby girl.

"This, Kristy, is my granddaughter, Elizabeth Dion."

I tilted my head trying to make sense of it.

"During the grief, my son began to spend time with Betty's sister. They married last year and this is my gift. I have to say I'm still angry, but I understand that Betty didn't mean for it to happen, and perhaps this miracle wouldn't be here."

Betty and Dion didn't need to die for the baby to come into this world, but it was a blessed gift in the wreckage of grief.

With a Little Help

Simon prided himself on being a helper. When most twelve-year-old boys wanted to either sleep in, play baseball, or spend their Saturdays in front of the television set, Simon would be busy doing errands for his parents and the neighbors. He didn't even care if they paid him, although most did. If not with money, it was with brownies or casseroles that he would take back home and it would just help his mom.

It was springtime and there was a lot of yard work to be done around his area. Mrs. Bacy asked him the week before if he'd help get the pool ready to open and Simon was more than excited. It would mean that once it was sparkly clean he would get to use it. His mom was irritated, though, and although it probably had nothing to do with him, she certainly took it out on him.

"We have enough to do over here, Simon. And Mrs. Bacy doesn't even use that pool anymore. She should just take it down anyhow," she complained. "And she's never even paid you."

"But I'll get to swim when it gets warmer, mom. I'll try and hurry and come home to help you with the chores around here, okay?"

Simon's mom didn't respond, just turned her back and began to scrub the dishes.

Simon didn't want to upset his mom, but he had an obligation that he needed to keep, so he jumped on his bicycle and raced a block over to where Mrs. Bacy was bringing out the hose and the pool chemicals. The cover was heavy, but he handled it by himself and just as he pulled it completely off and was ready to take a break, Mrs. Bacy's dog jumped in, and started to panic.

"Gus," Mrs. Bacy screamed. "Gus, come here." She raced around the pool trying to reach the Maltese, but Gus had gone under and wasn't coming up. It was hard to see with the leaves and gunk that colored the water, and before Mrs. Bacy could stop him, Simon jumped in. Nobody knew how, the water depth was only a bit over five feet, but Simon was found unresponsive at the bottom of the pool by paramedics, holding the lifeless body of the white fluffy dog.

Simon's mom was inconsolable with grief with the traumatic loss of her kind and gentle son. Her anger turned toward Mrs. Bacy, who felt horribly responsible and grieved herself.

"We have to move," Simon's mom Edna told her husband. "I can't drive by that house because all I see is his lifeless body in the front yard."

Simon's dad Wallace understood, he was doing his best trying to keep it together for everyone else. There were nights that he found himself laying in Simon's bed, though, crying to God to take him in exchange for his son. Begging God to have mercy. "Simon was a better person than I ever was. Just please take me."

Wallace knew that he was being ridiculous and that it was impossible, but Simon's death was ridiculous and senseless too.

I was having a small group session where I typically have six to ten people in my office and I make the connection with spirit. These sessions are healing, and although death is often filled with deep sadness, the groups tend to bond in an almost therapeutic way and we laugh, cry, and laugh some more. It was a small group when I met Edna and Wallace. It had been thirty years since Simon had passed and he was the first one to show up to talk to his parents.

Simon had been twelve years old when he passed, but he showed himself to me at the age he would be if he was still here—forty-two. His hair was short, the most unusual green eyes, and a bright smile that made his brown skin glisten. He was surrounded by a blue light.

"I'm so sorry they've lived so long with regrets," he apologized.

"What does he do? Is he ever with us? Can he hear me talk to him?" Edna rattled off a dozen more questions that haunted her all these years.

I asked Simon to share his story.

"I'm not sure how I died," he confessed. "I remember the pool and then I remember being surrounded by big balls of light and then realized I could talk to them, but in my head. Like I'm doing with you," he added. "Every light felt familiar to me, like an old friend. As I got closer to the orbs, they began to guide me away from what we call earth and into what I will call heaven. I was never afraid. I was never sad except at seeing my family sad, but it wasn't like a sadness that sits with you and stirs within you. It's there, but it's not. I was taken to a light that was the brightest light I've ever seen before, and this light told me that I was a helper and that was my purpose. I know that it seems that so many years have gone by, but for me it's like its mere seconds, not years. This blue light you see," he widened out his arms to expand the light as if on command, "I've taken the role of helping like the lights that assisted me."

"He helps souls cross?" Wallace asked.

"I do," Simon confirmed. "And one day I'll help my parents as they cross, but until then I hope I can help them heal and not feel so alone in this journey. Life doesn't have to be hell on earth."

"Easier said than done," Simon's mom huffed, crossing her arms.

"Wallowing in the grief zaps the good energy. It keeps the focus off of what really matters. Tell mom that I hear her. I hear her every single day when she cries. I hear her ask for the signs, that I do give her. And I hear her ask God why. I don't have all the answers, but I do know that although she may not understand the reason why I was taken, I have a purpose. I've helped souls cross over that never believed they deserved happiness. I've helped babies, and pets, and ninety-year-olds. I've shown them that they deserve to be loved and to love. As much as I know she wishes I could've done that with her, this is what it is."

I was a bit unsettled as I gave them the messages. Simon was very composed, as if he was the parent and they were the children. In a way, he was the teacher and we were the students.

"I know Grandma passed. She didn't want to add to your stress and she hung on hard and long. I came to her in the hospital and I told her I'd be with her through her journey. Did she tell you that?"

Edna looked up with tears sparkling in her eyes and nodded. "She told me she saw my son and that she was going to be with him. I thought maybe she was just trying to make me feel better. Are they together?"

Simon hesitated a moment. "We see one another and we are both in heaven, but Mom, c'mon, she's annoying."

Wallace didn't have a chance to swallow his water and spit it out, spraying several of the group and we all fell into giggles.

"Yep, that's Simon. He always said it like it was, and I also feel that my mother-in-law is annoying. Please tell me I don't have to spend eternity with her either."

Edna teasingly swatted Wallace on the shoulder, but joined in the laughter.

I've been told that we all have jobs, and I joke that when I get to heaven mine will just be resting and relaxing, something I don't do much here on earth. Simon was predestined, apparently, for his heaven role, and he took it very seriously.

Chapter Seven

Heaven Here,
Heaven There, Heaven Everywhere

Because everyone's heaven is different, just because certain people might show up together during a session or a visit doesn't mean they spend all their time together. We need help on earth, and often in the afterlife as well. The reasons aren't always explained, especially when several families are mourning at the same time. Recently there was a news story of a mother who died in a car crash and not even an hour later her young daughter was crossing the road and was hit and died. Growing up there was a young man who had a carefree spirit and a loving nature. It was that loving nature that ended his life. Someone asked him for a few dollars and as he reached into his pocked the person shot him. When the police came to tell his father, his father reached for his chest, had a heart attack and died right there in the doorway. I like to think that they found one another and assisted one another through the doorway of heaven.

Sally Lou

I spent many years mourning people from the past. Some people I knew, and some transitioned before my earthly time; this made me wonder if timelines somehow coincided.

It was something I inherited from my mom. The difference was I knew how to live in the now and make plans for the future. My mom often lived in grief of the past, not knowing how to move forward. It wasn't until she found her heavenly home that she found peace.

My mom, Sally Lou McLaughlin (Schiller), lived a fairly simple life. She would often tell me stories of her lack of toys, her fondness of music, and the love she had for her family. She was shy in social settings, but opinionated and intuitive. By the age of forty-one, she had lost her whole family, both brothers, her mom, and her dad, and she felt like an orphan. After that it was rare that she could see over the cloud of depression and sadness that wrapped tightly around her. "I wish there was family for you, Kristy," she would say to me. With my constant reply of, "But Mom, I just need this family." But for her, it wasn't enough. It wasn't how she pictured it.

Books were her escape and when her sight was taken from her, she seemed to lose everything that she ever loved, and told me that many times. Despite having my dad, me, my sister, and my brother, she couldn't move past all she had lost to see all that she had. And although there were many times I would get angry with her for sitting in the cloud of depression, exhausted by her negativity and worry, I couldn't; and I still can't judge her, because what she was going through was hers and nobody could fix it except for her. I didn't have the magic word or a potion that could bring back her family, her health, or her soul and spirit.

Two days before she passed away, I sat at her bedside holding her hand. "I want to go home ...," she told me as I told her how much I loved and missed her. I wiped back the tears with the back of my hand, trying hard to keep my voice from shaking. Swallowing my sobs, I reassured her that we were trying to get her home and soon. She squeezed my hand and whispered, "Not that home."

My mom started going blind when I was twelve. It was life-changing for us all and she felt like she was a burden most days. My mom never saw me in a prom dress. She never saw me walk down the church aisle to get married. She never saw what my kids looked like, or showed me how to put on makeup. Even though she was there, she wasn't there mentally—the blindness made her a manic depressant—and because of her vision issues, she felt like her presence didn't count anyhow. Although she never believed in herself even when she did have sight, she showed me how to fight through adversity and reminded me always to believe in me.

My mom always wanted a house by the sea. She dreamed of Maine (even though she had never visited there), loved an English or Irish accent, loved her historical romance novels, and adored jewelry. When she went blind, she would tell me that life was too short for itchy clothes or smelly people and to use all my senses and enjoy everything about life. She loved Cool Whip more than cake and lots of sparkles and bling despite not being able to see it. She always loved the sun rays on her skin, but had Lupus and had to wear long sleeves and a floppy hat. But she ached to sit by the water, toes in the sand, and a book in her hand, surrounded by hydrangeas and lilac bushes.

It would've been her eightieth birthday when she visited me in the early morning. She'd been gone eleven earthly years. She came to me looking young and bright eyed. I asked her how she was celebrating her birthday. Excitedly she told me she was going to see Neil Diamond in concert. I laughed and told her that he wasn't on the other side and she said she was just going to go haunt him at his house and we laughed. My mom rarely laughed or joked, and to hear her laugh was heaven in itself for me.

"So your heaven is in Neil Diamond's living room?" I joked.

My mom turned serious. "When we came to earth, we came from a place of nothing and we return to a place of nothing. God is everywhere, not any special place. You used to say church made you feel the furthest away from God, but for others that is where they feel the closest. Our souls are present everywhere and anywhere, yet nowhere."

When I woke up this morning I looked outside to see a female cardinal sitting there on the fence, looking up at my bedroom window and I said happy birthday to my mom again. I felt like it was a sign, a heaven hello. Something we are gifted with often but are too busy to notice, and yet they want to send their love from heaven.

Our loved ones on the other side want to send us reassurance, signs, and blessings. Are you paying attention to the license plate in front of you? Or the billboard with your loved one's name on it? Or the time that just so happened to be your birthdate, or another date that has meaning? These subtle signs are quite simply your love from heaven.

I'm sure that my mom's birthday was perfect, as is her heaven. She's surrounded by her family, who she missed dearly when she was here on earth. She's shown me that her heaven is happy, with an ocean breeze and her sitting on the porch of a quaint cottage surrounded by wildflowers, and no weeding to be done. And yes, Neil Diamond is her background soundtrack.

My mom was an old soul and her physical aches and pains were brought on by her soul aches and pains. She mourned for what never was, instead of trying to create a positive life. It's a hard lesson for old souls to know that dialing back the clock isn't the progression forward for the soul.

Chapter Eight

Old Souls and New Souls

Souls can volunteer to reincarnate into a journey that can make for difficult births, difficult lives, and/or difficult deaths. These are often called old souls. My own daughter Micaela fought to be here on this earthly plane. I was bedridden for days to weeks in pre-term labor with the threat of losing her. When I developed pre-eclampsia she was breech and in no way, shape, or form was coming into this world normally. An urgent cesarean required me to be in intensive care for several days, unable to bond with my blonde, blue-eyed beauty. Walking early, reading early, and getting frustrated with this life and all who try to control her—these are all symptoms of an old soul.

"Why do I feel so alone?" It's a question I'm frequently asked by clients, and it's a feeling I've felt in the depths of my own soul, which later in life I realized was a complication of being an old soul.

We are each like a tree and we have to nourish the trunk of the tree for the limbs to grow healthy. Sometimes the limbs of the tree need to be cut off in order for new growth to happen. These limbs could be past loves, friendships that only lasted a season, a job opportunity that didn't work out, a current love that is unhealthy, issues with family, financial problems and the list continues.

Old souls have a tendency to nourish everyone else. They help others with their work, but don't do their own work or allow others to help them out. The trunk that used to be so strong often becomes dry rotted from not allowing or accepting the proper nourishment.

Realizing that you are allowed to trim your limbs, care for your trunk—your very soul—strengthens every part of you. You are allowed to be strong, and when you aren't, allow someone to help you until you regain your soul strength. Just as the flight attendants remind us that we have to put our own oxygen on in an emergency before helping another, it is the same with life. You can help someone, but not before helping yourself. It's a difficult lesson for an old soul, because old souls are the helpers.

Traits of an Old Soul

- **Introverted**—Many old souls are introverted. They'd rather spend time with a few people than with many.
- **Love for Antiques/Classics**—Would much rather spend time and money on old gadgets than the newfound toys.
- **Interested in History**—History isn't something to be discarded according to old souls. It's its own textbook to study and learn from.

- **Fascination with an Era**—Much like the interest in history, old souls tend to be committed to a certain era, the music, the people, and even the clothing.

- **Learns Differently**—Old souls tend to learn differently, and can be frustrated in situations when told to do it a new way when the old way worked just as well.

- **Knowledge**—They often possess a deep seeded knowledge of information that was never learned, wisdom from before.

- **Love**—Old souls love deeper than new souls. They might fall harder than most, as they like to make connections worthwhile.

- **The Advisor**—Old souls are the advisors of their group of friends and family. No matter their age, they have the sage wisdom.

- **Overcomplicated**—Old souls are the thinkers, and they over-complicate everything in their minds. It's a spiritual form of ADD.

- **No Drama**—Often passive, old souls would much rather avoid the drama than create or dive into the drama.

- **Sensitive/Emotional**—Old souls feel everything—positive and negative. They value beauty, art, and music because they feel every piece of it. Along with this, they typically feel like their own feelings aren't important, and may feel guilty and apologize if feeling angry or sad.

- **Quiet, Please**—Old Souls flourish in a calm, loving, and peaceful environment. Because they feel everything, it can be damaging when they are surrounded by negative emotion. It can physically and emotionally hurt them. Often if the surroundings are less than perfect, they may have confusing physical symptoms that don't add up for a medical diagnosis.

- **Older Generations**—Old souls drink in the wisdom of the past generations. It feels familiar to them.

- **Givers**—Old Souls like to travel light in an emotional sense. Even though they hold on to so much in their mind, they would much rather live a simpler life filled with hope, love, peace, and pureness.

- **Admiration of Nature, Animals, and Children**—Old souls see the value in what feels closest to heaven, and for them it's nature, animals, and kids.

- **Healers**—Many old souls are the healers of the world, and no matter what profession they decide to choose, there's always a matter of healing and helping that is the subconscious reason for that choice.

Reincarnated souls feel they have it the worst, having to live potentially several lifetimes trying to analyze their past, their present, and their future. This sometimes causes depression and frustration in old souls as they don't feel like they fit in. The crowded world might feel lonely, but sometimes you simply need to adjust your focus, remove the cloaks you've been carrying for so long. Your soul may be hundreds, or millions, of years old. You may very well be a healer, and even healers need to take time to heal.

New Souls

On the other hand, there are the new souls. A new soul has a clean slate. Never reincarnating before, they draw knowledge and wisdom from the current lifetime. Some have referenced new souls to being the manipulators of this lifetime, but both old and new can fit that pattern. It's not that new souls are uncaring, egotistical beings; they just have more learning to do and can come across as *in the moment* type people. Often described as lacking common sense, a new soul has a hard time finishing projects and might worry over what an old soul considers silly.

Traits of a New Soul

- **Highly Competitive**—New souls are very competitive and want the fame and the fortune and will often do whatever necessary to get it.

- **Aims for Success**—New souls want to make a mark on the world, but often it comes at a price with friendships and family.

- **Opinionated**—New souls believe that their way is the right way, and often the *only* way.

- **Forever Young**—New souls are often concerned with their looks or their age.

- **Adventurers**—New souls are the explorers who take chances and try to constantly discover new paths.

- **Attracted to Old Souls**—New souls are confused and yet bewildered by old souls. These relationships are often spontaneous and can be damaging. This isn't simply romantic, but also parental, sibling, and friend. Opposites do attract, though.

New souls don't care to fit in and have a hard time understanding old souls who want so badly to belong. This can cause a lot of strife between the two souls. The infant soul, which is closest to the original state of heaven, continues to hold their past physical and heavenly experiences with connections to the other world. Old souls can become frustrated with having to do the same ole same ole all over again. New souls come to this world, never having lived before, and still hold on to the state of heaven. Chosen just the same, they are curious and even excited for new adventures. The old souls are the teachers, the new souls the students. Both have lessons to learn, though, and both are gifts to the experience. The old souls have to learn they don't know everything, and the new souls have to find their worthiness that they belong here too.

Souls and Gender

Gender traits can and have switched throughout the lifetimes. Those souls that were masculine in one lifetime can come through as another gender, but still have the masculine trait, or vice versa. If a soul switches gender, they may not fit into today's label and are often considered homosexual or transsexual. The fact remains, however, that no matter what label it is they are a human. The gender trait isn't gender based as much as personality based. These traits seem to appear lifetime to lifetime, from earth to heaven, hell, or in between. For instance, if you were quiet in this lifetime, you'll be quiet on the other side, and if you reincarnate you'll more than likely be quiet in the next life. There is an evolution and possibly a lesson in finding your voice, but that trait is part of who you are, much more so than blue eyes or brown hair.

The Gifted

Another aspect of an old soul that carries from one lifetime to the next, and even on to the afterlife, is of gifts, the hard-earned achievements that make us who we are. Spiritually and intellectually, we seem to pick up where we have left off. Child prodigies can be explained by reincarnation. The soul holds on to the information and talent and calls it into the physical body and mind of the next lifetime, and each lifetime after.

In her book *The Boy Who Knew Too Much*, Cathy Byrd discusses the incredible story of her son Christian Haupt. At the age of two he was a baseball prodigy who began sharing vivid memories of once being Lou Gehrig. The details were too great for a toddler to know or even understand, describing historical facts and even rivalries between other baseball legends. It wasn't just stories, it was the talent that he exhibited on the field as well. There are child prodigies who without one lesson sat down at the piano and played an incredibly difficult piece, to toddlers who can share intimate details of wars from long ago.

Old Soul, Today's Wounds

The past and the present are interwoven through birth defects, from one incarnation to the next. The defect is thought to be formed into the present incarnation as a reminder of where you came from, and that healing can take place.

My Micaela was born with her fire mark, or angel kiss as I called it. Some are born with heart defects, scars on different parts of their body, or birth defects. All of these are physical reminders from a past lifetime, with a present lesson.

Part Two

Hell

There are various theories as to what hell is and where it's located. Most believe hell to be a dark and foreboding place. In the New Testament, Hades, which means unseen, is a temporary abode before the judgement and eternal punishment. Popular culture depicts hell with a silly red devil, holding a pitchfork, telling people to get back to shoveling coal in a hot and steamy furnace-like location.

The King James version of Ephesians 4:9 says that before Jesus ascended into heaven "he also descended ... into the lower parts of the earth." Some have interpreted that as the center of the earth where the core reaches upwards of 12,000 degrees Fahrenheit. However, the New International translates it to "he also descended to the lower, earthly regions," meaning that Jesus came back to earth.

So is hell on earth? Or is it purgatory? Or are they one in the same? According to the Bible, hell is as real as heaven is. It's a place of everlasting contempt and guarded by the fallen angel, Lucifer—Latin for morning star or bringer of light—and his demons.

In the English versions of the New Testament, Hades wasn't referred to as a place of suffering and punishment at all. It's believed by many philosophers and theologists that the fire and brimstone concept of hell was a mere scare tactic. Hell was derived from Old English *hel* which refers to a nether world of the dead. Although still in conflict over what, where, or how, the Bible states that Christ suffered in hell so that believers wouldn't have to. Often times, it is our own mind that is our worst enemy, and not any actions. Some people feel as if hell is a tormented state of mind, something right here on earth. Often times we are personally involved in generating our own reality here on earth, so quite possibly we create our afterlife as well, which could make for a self-made nightmarish scenario. For me, hell resided in my own childhood home.

The Abyss

The house breathed in our energy and breathed out the worst of us.

The Detroit riots were a violent altercation that happened on July 23, 1967 and ended just days later with 43 dead, 1,189 injured, over 7,200 arrests, 300-plus families homeless, and more than 2,000 buildings destroyed. On November 13, 1970, I was brought home to what I thought looked like a quaint Victorian house in the northwest part of Detroit, also called Old Redford. At that time telephone exchanges had names much like street names. Rather than mere digits, you would share your telephone exchange and others would know what area you resided in. Mine was KENWOOD, today it's simply the 313 area code. Although the riots had ended three years before I was unexpectedly conceived, Detroit's great-

ness was all but gone, burned into ashes without the Greek mythological phoenix anywhere in sight to give hope for renewal.

My mom hated the house that my dad bought in the valley of
the Motor City. Although there were features of the house that
were flawed, it had nothing to do with cosmetic appearances. The
home was spiritually unsound, but nobody could quite put their
finger on what it was or even understood how it affected the family
dynamic. Yet, it did.

I was a colicky baby according to my parents, mostly calmed
only with a car ride. Doctors had no explanation for my constant
crying, and it was never witnessed since I never acted similarly outside of the house. Everything from a milk allergy to sleep deprivation was blamed, and yet nothing placated the screams unless I was
taken out of the home.

I was about three years old when I began seeing the energies.
Some were good. Most were bad. The good spirits would calm and
they would reassure me of their protection from my fears, the fears
that took shape. Sporadically seen in human shape, most would
stir the room with a black mist that moved into the darkest cor-
ners. There seemed to be no boundaries for the shadows. They
moved through walls, room to room. Their favorites were the
basement, my brother's room on the second floor, and a small
closet in the back of a room I shared with my sister.

The shadows would taunt and tease, grabbing at our ankles
with invisible frostiness from under the bed, jumping out from underneath the basement steps while we did laundry and creating
heart pounding panic. The worst was the emotional issues that
spun throughout the house. From rage to depression, it touched
everyone in the household in different ways.

Even though I had a lovely bedroom on the second floor, ninety percent of my nineteen years in that house was spent sleeping on the itchy plaid wool living room couch, nearest the front door and my parent's bedroom. My parents did everything to bribe me to stay in my bedroom from painting it my favorite color of purple to installing my own phone line, but it had nothing to do with being a spoiled brat it was just plain substantiated fear. When my brother and sister moved out, the energy shifted its target to terrorizing me. If I were to have to get up in the middle of the night to use the bathroom, I'd jump from the bed as close to the doorway as possible, leap past my brother's old room and into the bathroom, and repeat. Most nights I would stay wide awake, falling asleep at dawn, comfortable in knowing that the shadows had also gone to rest. I was exhausted. The phone line that my parents had installed would ring in the middle of the night with voices asking for me by name. "It must be the wrong number, or someone from school," my mom would reason. And yet the phone number would never come up on the bill to substantiate her logic. One night even my parents woke up. The clock radio in my brother's room blinked three o'clock in the morning when a booming laugh sounded through the speakers.

My mom yelled up to me, "Turn it off!" There was no turning it off, though. It wasn't the radio, it was the energy. My dad unplugged the radio only for it to continue with a deep laughter of mocking.

"I'll always win," the voice warned before it quieted.

Invitations for sleep overs to my home were almost always rejected, and those that accepted would leave in the middle of the night, scared or ill. It wasn't until several years ago when I reunited with them via social media and they explained that their dismissal of hanging out with me had nothing to do with me, but the house.

"You do know that your house was haunted, right?" One childhood friend explained, wide eyed, as we met over lunch.

I wasn't sure whether to sob or hug her with the validation. I did know, though. So did my whole family.

My dad intently studied the Bible, and it was his sparked curiosity that triggered unimaginable encounters we had with evil entities from the darker realm. His interest peaked when he received a flyer about a Presbyterian minister who did missionary work in Third World countries. His lecture would be on his specialty—exorcism. With a tape recorder and me, all of nine-years-old, in tow, we sat down in the pew to listen and watch a video of his documentary.

I found the minister charismatic. Dressed in a light-colored button-down shirt and casual slacks, his smile was friendly. He wasn't at all what I had imagined a demon hunter would be like. He began his lecture and then stopped after about ten minutes in.

"We forgot to pray," he gasped. "We must pray in order to protect ourselves and to ask God to allow the recordings to work."

The minister said a quick prayer and began again. The lecture, probably no more than an hour long, was absolutely fascinating. He showed slides of exorcisms he'd done, and explained that hell was in fact walking and breathing among all of us.

When we got home my dad rewound the cassette tape and hit play. We heard moans, howls and screams of unknown origin and then we heard the minister loudly say *amen*, and the tape played perfectly.

Just a few nights after that lecture I awoke to a man's voice distinctly coming through my alarm clock radio. He called my name and laughed as I pulled my legs up to my chest, frightened. I recited "The Lord's Prayer," asking him to go away, but asking isn't always effective. The entity continued to haunt my family until my father burned all the material that had to do with devils and demons.

Around the same time my dad had taken interest in hell, my siblings decided it would be fun to play with a Ouija board. It was a perfect storm for chaos to ensue.

Although things quieted down, the fear was very much planted. I begged for my dad to put the house up for sale. My mom endlessly pleaded for the same, but my dad was a proud man. A veteran. Union auto worker. Hard worker. No ghost was going to push him out of his house. Even after the furnace unexplainably exploded as he lit the pilot light sending him to the hospital with severe burns, he still wouldn't budge. It would take an attempted burglary for my parents to finally move, and that was after I married and had kids.

The day they moved I stayed at their new house waiting for the moving van.

"You don't want to say goodbye to the house?" my dad asked.

There was no sentimentality. I felt as if the energy within that home stole the joy out of my childhood. It literally stole my mother's sight, with unexplained blindness and various health issues. With that it stole my mother as a whole. It tried to steal my dad with peculiar accidents that very well could have and should have been deadly. It pushed my sister out of the house at a very young age, as arguments were heated and common. No, there was no saying goodbye to that house, there was only the celebration that my parents were finally leaving. I only wished it had happened before the physical and emotional scars that marked me and each one of my family members: ghastly souvenirs.

The nightmares began immediately after my parent's move, each one different but frightening all the same. The house seemed to have a hold on me and no amount of forgetting or distance separated the energy connection. I'd wake up remembering that I was safe and not there. I could get up in the middle of the night and not worry that something was carefully watching me. I could light a candle, assured that the glass wouldn't shatter with an attempt to harm me. I was safe. One thing it was doing was trying to deprive me of my sleep in order to seed the doubts of that safety.

It had been over twenty years since my parents moved away, but the dreams of the old house were still happening weekly. Most of the dreams were me trying to find my parents in the house, or being locked in the home, and some just revisited the past memories like a home movie playing. I pretended to interpret the dreams in a symbolic way, until trepidation of the past turned into true reality.

"Kristy!"

Even though it was negative temperatures outside, and the furnace was on the nighttime timer of sixty-eight degrees, my sweat-stained night clothes clung to me.

"What's wrong?" I opened my eyes confused, sitting straight up in bed. My husband Chuck stood on my side of the bed starting down at me. My heart was still palpitating from the vision, so real that my curled hand could still feel the cold blood. I was afraid it would be stained.

"You were screaming. You okay?"

Physically, I was fine.

"Can I tell you about this dream?"

I had night visitors, visions, and dreams frequently. Most of the time it was just plain weird like something out of a M. Night Shyamalan film. This was more real. I was waiting for Chuck to tell me to just go back to sleep like he normally did, but instead he climbed back into bed and took hold of my hand.

———

The house was alit even though it was well after midnight. The two young men stood facing one another. The silence was fraught as the anticipation hung thickly in the air, each one awaiting the first move.

The dark shadows that taunted me for years danced around the men. I wondered why they couldn't see me. Why couldn't they feel me? Was I a shadow too?

It happened all too quickly, the taller of the men grabbed the other by the neck and with a knife I hadn't seen before now began stabbing him. First in the neck, and then in the chest, over and over until they both fell to the ground.

"I'm your brother. I love you," the dying man cried, gasping for air that couldn't possibly fill up his damaged lungs.

The murderer dropped the knife and looked down on his brother in surprise, as if just coming upon him for the first time. Then he ran. The familiar noise of the screen door shutting behind him was surreal as I knelt beside the lifeless body. The blood pooled on the tan carpeting and I checked for a pulse, but there was none. I had to get out. The shadows lurked closer as the man's soul began to rise from his physical body and it was then that he saw me.

"Stay away," he whispered to me. "Far away."

It was then that Chuck nudged me awake.

———

"It can easily be checked out," Chuck rationalized. "You know your street address and you can check police reports. It's probably just another nightmare, though, Kristy."

It didn't feel like just a night terror, and sleep wasn't going to come gently. Maybe for a long time.

I tried to shake the nightmare, but memories of the home began to evolve like post-traumatic stress. The bug infestations. The birds that made their way in. The man that showed up at our door one summer night holding an axe, only to disappear into the night when my mom screamed. Hundreds of traumatic and terrible memories that I thought I'd boxed up and burned were found and plopped right there at my feet to deal with.

So I sat at the computer, trying to prepare myself for just being crazy. I just have an active imagination, I said giving myself a pep talk. I'm a writer, after all. I bleed on paper, and then bleed myself more to see if it changes. It's the curious nature of an artist. So maybe this was simply my way of working out a traumatic childhood. Maybe there were no demons or darkness, just depression and sadness. Maybe.

After some digging, though, I discovered that the nightmare wasn't a made-up scenario, but instead was very real and true.

Marco and Juan's parents passed away within months of one another from cancer. Marco, nineteen years old, responsible with a good job was given temporary custody of Juan who was sixteen at the time of his parent's death. Marco's personality began to slowly evolve from the quiet and pleasant young man everyone recognized to brooding and quick to anger. Family and friends believed it was that he was still grieving and stressed with the newfound responsibilities, but others were concerned. After his parents passed he began to meet up with a group some believed were practicing dark arts. Some said they were Satanists pretending to be Wiccans. Juan was confused because they'd been raised Christian and he didn't understand this newfound interest in black magic.

It wasn't that he was interested, it was that the shadows had found someone who was vulnerable and took advantage of Marco, and both Juan and he would ultimately suffer.

Marco pled guilty and was given twenty years of life in an Indiana prison.

I found the newest homeowner on social media and, after some meditating and praying, decided to contact her, asking if she had ever experienced any paranormal occurrences, not knowing what my future plans would be if she did. "Never," she responded.

The laughter of the entity sometimes still sounds in my head, like the vibration of speakers after a concert. The entity may have gone back into hibernation after Juan's murder, or quite possibly followed Marco, leeching onto him into the prison system to feed on lower vibrational people.

Because of my childhood experience, when I began this work as a psychic medium I decided to not resonate with any low vibrations. In other words, I just don't dial the phone to hell. I threw away the number. But it seems some beings from hell still have me on speed dial.

Charlene

It was a sunny July afternoon when I laid down for a quick nap. How is it that when we are younger we don't want to sleep, and as we get older naps become more glorious but sleep just doesn't seem to come? I had several clients that morning and was hosting a large gallery event that evening and felt like I needed some rest, but instead of visiting slumber, Charlene showed up.

Charlene had a short blonde pixie cut and bright blue eyes. She was fast to apologize for bothering me, but she wasn't sorry enough to leave. Instead, she sat down on the end of the bed and began chatting.

"My daughter is coming tonight. She's not really a believer, though," she rolled her eyes. "Kimmy, her best friend is bringing her in hopes I show up. Well, I'm always there but I marked it on my calendar to be as loud as I could. Not that I ever had a problem with that," she laughed.

"I didn't want to leave my family. In fact, I was the glue that held them together and I was incredibly concerned that they would fall apart," she reminisced. "But I closed my eyes and when I opened them I saw family I've missed for so long welcoming me, including Missy, my Golden Retriever. I cried, I was so happy. It wasn't that I forgot my family on earth, but it was as if I had awakened. I used to joke that Santa could see all and at that moment I felt as magical as Santa Claus. I can't always be with my family here, but I can guide and watch over them."

There was no need to prompt Charlene, she was happy to keep chatting.

"The hospital room felt full, but it was just my daughter by my bedside at that moment. The nurse was checking my vitals every so often. I really wanted to be at home, but I never got there. The cancer diagnosis was just a few months before. Pancreatic cancer. I never drank anything harder than iced tea. I remember telling the doctor that when he called me into his office with the news. He gave me six months tops. He should be a psychic himself because it was six months and one day. I was always a bit of a wannabe rebel," she laughed.

"Did you get a life review?" I asked, curiously.

"It was right after my reunion. During my life review I was asked what I wanted my heaven to be. It was like being a kid in a candy shop. I could choose whatever it was I wanted, they told me. My most favorite trip was my twentieth anniversary with my husband. He took me to Hawaii. The people were the friendliest I've ever encountered, and the landscape, well, it was breathtaking. We renewed our vows on that trip. I'd never felt more peaceful," she heavily sighed.

"So that's your heaven?"

"Most times." She smiled mischievously. "I was united with my husband and my heaven and his heaven are different. I'd rather be surrounded by water and he'd rather be inside watching television, paying attention to the world happenings. So we compromised there."

"But you're together?"

"We are. For eternity. We loved one another unconditionally. Most can't say that."

It was easy to spot Charlene's daughter in the audience of the gallery session. Not only did she emit the same energy of her mom, but physically she was a carbon copy.

"You must be Charlene's daughter," I said, stepping off the stage and walking through the aisle until I was in front of her. She looked at me skeptically, and then I shared my visit with her mom. It wasn't until I mentioned Missy their dog when the tears began.

"She's good. She's made it to her heaven, which is sometimes with your dad, and sometimes with a pool boy," I joked and everyone laughed including Charlene's daughter and friend.

Charlene lived an authentic life here, and because of it she's able to enjoy her heaven without the baggage of doubt and fear.

Chapter Nine

They'll Find You

It was a chilly autumn afternoon in October at one of the most beautiful places in Michigan—Mackinac Island. I was there for business, but even on business I try to find time to explore, and that is what I was doing along with several of my friends, my husband, and my son. The streets were crowded with tourists, and we were hungry so we first dined at the Pink Pony for an early dinner. Then, stopping in a fudge shop, we taste tested a few before purchasing our favorite choices, along with some taffy to enjoy as dessert later on in the hotel.

Mackinac Island was founded in 1670 and the only way to get to this summer retreat is by small plane or ferry (the most popular means). You won't find automobiles on this island either. To make your way around you can bring or rent bicycles, take a horse and carriage ride or lace up your sneakers and walk it. The circumference is just eight miles, but most of the restaurants and lodging are along the main street. Two battles took place on the Island; the fort is still standing and open for tours. It is notable for the filming of the 1980 movie *Somewhere in Time* with Christopher Reeve and Jane Seymour. Once you step foot on Mackinac Island you really do feel as if you've stepped back in time, and the beauty of Lake Huron makes you ache to stay. At least until winter comes. Maybe it's the beauty along with the reminiscence of simpler times why so many spirits haven't left either. So no matter where you stay, you might encounter a haunting or two, or something more.

I had brought ghost seekers with me, with events to help them get into the Halloween spirit. Ghost walks and investigations were on the haunting menu, but we had a day beforehand to explore for ourselves. For some reason I thought it was also a good idea to book Chuck, Connor, and I into the most haunted room at Mission Point hotel to add to our paranormal excursions.

Since we had a group of familiar people—all excited for their getaway and hopefully some ghostly encounters and seeing, as Mackinac Island is so small—there were continuous greetings being shouted across the street to one another. As I exited one of the many souvenir shops with my small group, I heard my name being called and was surprised to see that it was someone I worked with over a decade ago. *What a small world it really was*, I thought. We chatted a bit, and said our goodbyes. When I turned around my husband, son, and friends had all disappeared. I glanced across the street to see if I could catch sight of anybody recognizable, but I discovered that I was abandoned. As I reached into my purse to dig out my phone I felt as if someone was watching me. Turning around, I saw a child, about ten years old, wearing a long brown wool coat and a matching flat cap.

"How are you today, ma'am?" the voice asked.

Surely, the kid must've mistaken me for someone else, but then he repeated it. "How are you today, ma'am?"

I felt bound to the ground, unable to speak. Not only was this boy's dress interesting, his eyes were hypnotic and colored entirely black. I shivered and with all my effort took a step back from him.

"I'm fine," I whispered, surprised that I had no voice.

The boy looked hard at me for a second in seriousness. "Remember they'll always find you. There's no hiding from your past." He offered a quick smile before running up the street in the direction of our hotel.

Despite being afraid, my curiosity and confusion decided that I needed to follow him, but he disappeared into the crowd, which had reappeared. Standing in a haze in the middle of the street I heard a more familiar voice call my name and saw my husband.

I must've looked as shocked as I felt because he asked me if I was okay. Trying to shake the experience, I told him I was.

This may seem like such an innocent encounter, but it was different. This kid was different, he wasn't of this dimension.

"Well, that's a Black-Eyed Child," a friend in the paranormal explained after I shared my encounter.

I scoffed. BEKs are just fables, simple lore, right?

Black-Eyed People (sometimes called Black-Eyed Children or BEK) are classified as young people, often children, who have eyes that are solid black with no differentiation between sclera, pupil, or iris. Some have noted that their skin color is tinted blue, as if they are a corpse. They sometimes appear in pairs and their mannerisms are confident and even eloquent, with speech patterns of an adult. But who are they, and what do they want?

One paranormal explorer told me she thought they were aliens, or non-entities, possibly demonic. "They try and get into our head, your mind, your soul and your heart. It conjures images of vampire lore. You have to invite them into your house, job, life, or car—but don't," she said. "Whatever they are, they are soul suckers."

Creepy. But this kid I ran into simply was checking up on me, I told her. No harm, no foul. Right?

"And yet you're shivering reliving that moment," she noted.

I was. I still do.

"And seriously, why was he checking on you?" she continued.

I didn't have an answer then and I still don't. Why me? Why then? Why there? And what the heck?

Can I say for sure that I had an encounter with a Black-Eyed Child? I just don't know. I wish I could say that I had a drink or two, but I didn't. I wish I could say it was a ghost or spirit, that seems more realistic than this. I know that it wasn't.

Mackinac Island, one of the most beautiful places I've explored, certainly has its share of legends, hauntings, and unknowns, so why not add BEK to it? The Island, surrounded by water, which is a conduit for spirit activity, has seen its share of violence, murder, and mystery through the years. It's believed by many that demons, or negative entities, reveal themselves through paranormal activity so that people will delve further into the curiosity. The attraction can draw a soul further away from good, in order to explore the negative.

The next two nights in our hotel room, my family had several paranormal experiences that weren't pleasant. From being pulled off the bed, to our hair being pulled, to objects missing, and my husband even waking up to an entity snuggling with him that had him jumping out of bed as fast as could be. A warning from the boy, possibly, about the hotel, or a deep message on life.

Just as we all have endless personalities as mankind, so do those on the other side, the good and the evil. Negative energies are the rejected ones. It doesn't mean that they look like green goblins or red devils. When we go into the afterlife our age is our soul maturity, not necessarily the age of death. I felt that this innocent looking child, with his ominous message, was testing my strength and belief system.

Another friend who was a non-entity curator once told me that the more you seek, the more you find, and to always be careful even, on your toes. It was a few months before he passed when he took me aside with some advice.

"Kristy, hell is all around us. It's not a place. It coincides and tries to magnetize us to it. Stay light. The darker you are, the easier it can creep in and the more it tries to snuff out your brightness. You always say you've lost the phone number to hell? Just break the phone altogether. Heaven can find you, hell will have a harder time."

Burt passed from cancer soon after he gave me my lesson, and just a couple months after my Mackinac Island experience. It only took him a month after his passing to find me.

"Heaven is amazing," he told me. "For most of my earthly life I explored hell and the unknown dimensions. I explored death, and the afterlife all the while forgetting that I should've been living. I got it now. I know we often have to have the personal experience in order to get it, but I hope you'll be careful and take time with the living more than the dead."

Whether it was my Mackinac Island experience or Burt's advice, I decided to choose my paranormal excursions and investigations carefully, spending my time more with the living than with the afterlife.

Chapter Ten

No Visiting Hours

A heavy heart is easily hidden, but a hardened heart is easily seen, and so often we harden ourselves through disallowing ourselves to forget, to forgive, and move on.

"I don't want to speak to him," she argued. "You weren't invited, Dad. Move along now," she called out, wringing her hands in her lap.

I thought she was about to bolt but thankfully her mom stepped forward, almost as if she was standing in another room.

"I'm not with him anymore, Charise. I've finally found my heaven," her mom said, caressing her daughter's hair.

Charise sat back in her seat, beginning to calm, swatting at her hair. "Do you promise me? Is Mom okay?" she began to cry.

"I promise. She's stroking your hair right now."

She put her hand back up to her head as if to grab on to her mom by the hand and let out a breath of relief.

A terribly abusive marriage resulted in Charise's dad murdering her mom and pulling the trigger, killing himself.

"I don't remember one day that my mom wasn't in fear for her life," Charise shared.

———

Troy and Lucy's marriage was rocky from the very beginning. High school sweethearts, Troy left for the military right after high school and although Lucy wanted to go to college, Troy had her working for his dad in his plumbing business as a secretary. Within a couple years while Troy was on leave they got married in the afternoon of a late September day. That evening as they sat outside the family cottage on their honeymoon, Lucy listened to the rattle of the cicadas on the horizon of autumn. Summer was almost done, and although it was her wedding day, she felt forlorn. The magic she thought she would feel was missing. The scent of burned leaves on the Saturday evening brewed anxiety, as if her own plight hung on to the sunset in the ashes of the nearby campfire.

Misadventures, fireflies, and a full moon created a chaotic oath as the clouds swept in and the moon peeked, quietly shedding just a flicker of light, but the darkness of confusion lingered.

Troy never liked her introspective personality, which was really just her, and on their wedding night he shared that dislike with a wedding gift of a shiner on her left eye. His right hook was the best according to his buddies. His wife would soon find out how talented he was too.

After the military, Troy became a police officer, working his way up the ranks to sergeant. Two kids—a boy and a girl—and twenty years later, he retired from the force. It was the evening after his retirement celebration when he was cornered by his family, or at least that's how he said he felt.

"Mom's leaving you," Evan, his son, flatly told him as they gathered in the great room of their childhood home.

"Right," Troy jested, popping open a can of beer.

"Mom, grab your bags," Charise instructed, turning the tables on the parenting roles.

"She'll be back, she always comes back," Troy laughed, taking one big gulp and finishing his drink, and opening another.

This was the third time that Charise and Evan had moved their mom out, and they hoped it would be the final. They'd watched her live her own personal hell with the constant beatings. The pendulum of life has varying degrees, ebbs, flows, and is sporadic and unpredictable. It's no wonder we sometimes lose our footing, but Lucy had been kept a prisoner and the kids would have no more. Lucy hadn't just lost her footing, she was losing her will and Charise and Evan couldn't help but try to change that.

Lucy was afraid for her life. Her husband's temper had grown more violent as time moved forward. The week before, Lucy woke to him choking her in his sleep.

"It's more than post-traumatic stress, Mom. That's his excuse. He needs help any which way and he won't get help," Evan had told Lucy the morning after the incident.

"Who you going to call?" Troy would say. "I am the police and nobody will believe you anymore. You're a lying piece of crap and everyone knows it. Nobody wants you, they never did. I should get a trophy for taking care of you. Look, there's nothing you ever need and yet you never appreciate anything I do."

She didn't know if the words hurt more or the beatings. At this point she felt numb. She didn't want to get him into trouble at work, so she just let it go, covering her wounds with makeup and her emotional hurt by writing poetry.

"Mom, he's killing you. You're slowly dying," Charise said, trying to quiet the thunder of anger that she felt about her father. Picking up the last piece of luggage she set it in her trunk.

"I'm worried about him, though," Lucy pursed her lips and looked back at the house. Her husband stood in the picture window, arms crossed, and a smug look on his face. He mouthed to her "You'll be back" and walked away, most likely to get a stiffer drink than the beer.

Charise and Evan tried with all their might to keep Lucy busy. They took her to the divorce attorney and drew up the paperwork. They went house shopping and found her a small home just a few miles from them. Lucy even went to the senior citizen hall and started to join various activities. She discovered that maybe she wasn't an introvert after all. Maybe Troy made her into an introvert. Or maybe she just didn't want to explain her bruises and scars. Now she was wearing them like a warrior. She survived, and although she wasn't about to take out a billboard announcing her abuse, she wasn't going to hide away anymore.

"I think I'm going to get a rescue puppy," she said. "Dad won't give me Buster. I've never had anything all my own."

Charise and Evan was amazed at how upbeat their mom was outside of the shadows of their father.

The final divorce papers were drawn up after a several month fight, constant texts and calls from her husband, and even a restraining order that Charise made her get. The fatal mistake came the day before the divorce hearing, when her ex asked her to come to the house to get the rest of her things and to sign a paper with regards to the home.

"I'll come when Charise gets off of work," she told him.

"Please, Lucy. Let's just get this sorted out," he said to her with a hint of agitation mixed with sorrow.

He sounded so sad, and sober at that, so reluctantly she told him she'd be over within the hour. Like many victims of domestic abuse, she believed he'd changed and she let her guard down.

As soon as Lucy was in the house, Troy locked the door and backed her into the corner.

"You've made me out to be a fool and I want you to feel how I feel." Taking his hand gun he shot at Buster, the dog, killing him immediately. Lucy screamed and in a rage, pushed Troy hard. Surprised, he took a step back and stared at her.

"They say till death."

At close range, Troy shot Lucy in the head. The lemon yellow walls were marked with blood. Without hesitation, Troy lay down next to her, held her hand, and shot himself.

———

"I found them both," Charise shook her head. "I don't know if I'll ever forget. The walls were covered in blood. The carpet soaked. He didn't even call 911 beforehand. He always wanted the last word, to be in charge. It had to be his way." Charise's face turned a splotchy pink. "I'm not sure I can cry anymore. The well has all dried up."

I could obviously see why she didn't want to speak to her father, and I was confused how or why he showed up to begin with.

As I looked deeper, I could see that her father didn't appear to be in the middle, he appeared to be in hell.

"Tell me he's burning in hell. Tell me he's living out his judgement in ugly eternity," she coughed.

"There's no excuse," he told me. "But when I was a child I was beaten and in school I was molested by a priest who was supposed to protect me. I guess I thought that what I was doing was normal."

I found it to be a pathetic excuse. He knew better. He was trained to serve and protect, and yet he couldn't even do that for his family," her eyes flickered with anger.

"Is it fire and brimstone?" I asked him, curiously.

Troy cleared his throat nervously and I caught a shadow of terror before he started.

"After I felt the pain in my head, I woke up in what I can only describe as a movie theatre where my entire life unfolded right in front of me. Every person I ever had contact with, I didn't just see them, I felt every emotion our interaction had on them.

"Once I did this life review I found myself in a large open field, and there I could see millions of sad souls wandering, in their own journey of anguish, consumed by their pain and misery of their life. And I realized then that in heaven you are alive, and in hell you die. There is no more of you. Dante called hell the inferno, but it's symbolic. It's not the fire and brimstone that is preached about, at least for me. For me it's a black hole of mistakes and regrets and that is where I dwell."

"Can you choose otherwise?"

"I've made my choices in life," he told me. "There's no visiting hours in hell."

If there's no visiting hours in hell then I was wondering how he was standing in front of me and talking.

I never did get my answer as to how I was able to connect with him. Like a hologram, he fizzled away as Lucy stepped forward.

Lucy, on the other hand, was enjoying her own paradise. She'd already lived her hell on earth.

"Your mom is free," I reassured her. "Just make certain to not awaken your own personal demons and get caught up in your own hell from this situation."

She started to argue and then stopped. "You're saying I have to forgive."

"I can't tell you to forgive. I can only tell you that the past can't be changed, but it can change you. Be careful that it isn't into the darkness."

———

A year later Charise shared a letter with me that she wrote to her father on the other side. It wasn't a pleasant read, as it outlined terrible things that he'd not just done to her mother, but to her as well. "Can you help me release this hurt?" she asked. We went outside my office and with a flick of a lighter, we lit the letter on fire, watching it burn.

"Imagine all your hate for him burning up with the letter, I told her. He has no more control over you, or your mom. This will help Mom enjoy her heaven too," I assured her.

After the letter burned up, I watched her walk to her car, her shoulders relaxed and her walk lighter. Her mom's spirit sat in the passenger seat, smiling. It was unfortunate she had to pass in order to find her release, but it wasn't too late for Charise.

Hell and heaven don't seem to intersect. There's no lobby where they can congregate or socialize with one another. Choices have been made, and it's locked in. The in-between sometimes intersects with both, as they make their decision and wrestle with their afterlife paths during their soul review.

Hell is a state of mind, self-imposed, and filled with the wrongs you've never forgiven yourself for. Your hell can be here on earth like Lucy's was, and it can last eternally if you let it.

We have all lived our own hell in life, and our own paradise. Once the soul departs the physical body, the soul joins the vibration that it most resonates with. Hell, according to Charise's father, wasn't a place. He said he lived a hell on earth, and never saw a light through the darkness so that is where he sits now—his own personal hell.

A Grave Matter

After the death of her husband, Glennis Wells was ready for a new beginning. Looking for calm and a slow pace, she found a property in a small rural town in western Michigan. She and her son Kinley were more than excited to start anew.

When the realtor showed her the eighteenth century farmhouse, colored sweet tea, just outside of town, she was already decorating in her mind. She would love the town, the realtor told her. A town with friendly country folks, and yes, there was several locations where she could eventually open her antique shop she always wanted to do, but until then the pole barn would suffice to store her treasures. It was her first official purchase since she was single, twenty something years before. She signed on the dotted lines and the next weekend she and Kinley began to move in.

Glennis was originally from a small village in Germany, and it was there that she met her husband, Frederick. They fell in love, got married, and soon afterward they were brought to Michigan due to his work in the auto industry.

Frederick worked long hours, but Glennis wasn't raised to be high maintenance. Instead, she kept busy with restoring old furniture and volunteering at the local church. She missed her family at home tremendously, but plane tickets were costly and Frederick was frugal. Most of the furniture she found came from the side of the road on trash day. Glennis never knew true love until she held Kinley and her life felt complete.

Not happy—that was different. She wasn't raised to be happy. She wasn't particularly happy in her marriage, or with Frederick in general. She knew he had women on the side, and that his dealings weren't always on the up and up. She was raised, though, to support her husband and be the best mother, and as long as nobody was being hurt, that life was good. Well, she was hurt some nights when she saw her husband texting from his home office, knowing that at midnight he would be called in by his work, but she decided to channel her attention to what did make her happy.

It was a strangely cold day for August when Frederick came home early from work. That in itself was strange, as Frederick rarely came home before seven in the evening. Seeing the car in the driveway, she quickly began supper. She was unprepared, having found a new table to paint; she'd been busy planning what she wanted to do with it as Kinley contently watched television and busily played with his building blocks.

"Sit down with me," Frederick asked after hanging up his suit coat.

"I will after I get this pasta to a boil," Glennis fretted, but Frederick took her hand and guided her to a seat.

"I'm dying, Glennis. The doctor says even with treatment I have just a few months. We need to get life in order now."

It began with what he thought was the stomach flu, but then nobody else got it in the house, and it lingered. Not loving doctors, it was finally the sharp pains in his side that warranted a doctor's visit. An order for various tests from ultrasounds to a CT Scan showed a mass in Frederick's liver, and there was more than likely cancer elsewhere according to his doctor, and there was. The diagnosis was stage four colon cancer with spots that spread to the liver and to the lungs, threatening to trail up to the brain.

"There's no treatment?" Glennis asked, shocked. She didn't even know he'd gone to the doctor.

Frederick sadly shook his head. "It's inoperable and chemo will buy me a month or two, but require hospital stays and surgeries, and other horrific procedures that simply won't matter. The end result will be the same. I've been sent home to die."

Like some universal joke, the radio began to play Tim McGraw's song "Live Like You Were Dying." Frederick died like he lived, unhappily. Of course he was in pain, Glennis understood that, but she thought he might want to hold their son or spend time with her, but instead he spent his days and nights in the darkness of his home office staring at the blank walls calling on death to take him.

Glennis heard a moan and a loud thump in the middle of the night and ran down to find Frederick had gotten his wish. Death came at three a.m. on October 30th, just a bit over two months after his diagnosis.

She hadn't told him her plans with the house. He hadn't asked, nor did he bother to care. When she retrieved his paperwork from the safe and took it to the attorney she found out that Frederick had another family all together, and he'd left the majority of his funds to the other woman and their two children. She was given the house that she didn't even want in a country that wasn't even home, but she made it home because of her husband.

The so-called family house went up for sale the day after the findings and sold within a month after, to her relief.

Glennis, a proud and private woman, didn't like asking anyone for help. She got the moving truck, and with a four-year-old in tow, moved into her new house all by herself.

It was the week after when she began to feel visited and wondered if the house was haunted or if Frederick had found them from beyond.

Glennis received my name and contact from someone at her church, and she asked if I'd visit her.

For wanting to move far away, she only moved less than ten miles from the marital home. It was less than a month since her move when I sat in her living room. As she ran to get us some tea, I looked around at the pristine home filled with tasteful, but minimal, furnishings. There were no photos and hardly any decorations, and yet there was heaviness in the energy that was hard to ignore.

Handing me a china tea cup filled with tea with a sugar cube on the saucer, Glennis sat across from me.

"Thank you so much for coming. I honestly had no idea who to turn to," she nervously stirred her sugar cube in her cup with a small spoon. "You were my last hope before seeing a psychiatrist."

Glennis stiffened, swallowing back her tears, she looked hard at me. "Do you think I'm going crazy?"

Behind every ghost is a story with different motivations. Just as we here are attracted to our earthly comforts, ghosts seek out the same. I could see a dark shadow standing still in the corner. The energy was ominous, like the calm in the eye of a hurricane. Before I could turn to respond to her question, my mind turned noisy and it made me grab my head.

"You hear him too?" Glennis exclaimed, rushing over to me.

It wasn't about hearing him, it was more about feeling him and his pain.

I am doomed for a certain term to walk the night. And for the day confined to fast in fires, till the foul crimes done in my days of nature are burnt and purged away. But that I am forbid to tell the secrets of my prison house. I could tell you stories that would slice through your soul, freeze your blood.

"Hamlet," Glennis muttered out loud.

We both heard him quote the ghost from Hamlet in our heads, and I wished I paid more attention to my college Shakespeare class.

"What of his do you have here?"

"I have nothing. I sent it to his other family to deal with."

Frederick's energy swirled closer to us and we both gasped for air.

Ashes to ashes, dust to dust, but my spirit isn't done living.

He was mocking us.

"His remains? Where are they?"

Glennis' face turned red in embarrassment. "I never picked them up from the funeral home."

Finality is something important for ghosts and Glennis thought that simply moving would move her away from the past, but without closure the past caught up.

"We have to send his soul away from you. Literally, this is a grave matter."

Glennis nodded. "I just don't think it's fair for him to find peace and for my son and I to not," she frowned.

"It's not up to you to rule on the judgement, as hard as that sounds."

After a brief car ride with her, we arrived at the funeral home. The home felt like it was swallowing us, and filled with static. Glennis collected the plain wooden box, and, with it in her lap, began to cry. I let her sob, scream, and swear out all of her pain and sadness without comforting her. It was her right of passage to feel all her feelings.

"What now?" she asked me, blowing her nose into a handkerchief. "What does he want me to do now?"

"No," I said harder than I wanted. "This has nothing to do with what he wants, but what you want. You are taking yourself back right now. You are giving you and your son a life back. You are sending him to his grave. You are decorating your home. You are releasing the chains right now.

"Take a right there, please, and go down to the lake's edge."

Following her directions we stopped behind a giant tree that blocked out the sunshine.

"Do you want me to come with you?"

Glennis shook her head no, and got out of the car with the box. I watched her walk to the shore of the lake, and, box and all, she threw it as far as she could. "In God's name, bless your soul," she cried.

The box bobbed before it disappeared. Glennis straightened her spine, letting out a sigh, she got back into the car.

"You okay?" I asked her.

It was the first smile I'd seen on her.

"I don't wish hell on him, you know. I really don't."

"No, I know. His actions were his own doing and all you can do now is to heal."

I parked the car in front of the home that immediately felt lighter. Walking in, the temperature felt cooler, and there were no more dark shadows.

It was a year later when Glennis invited me to her home, this time for a simple social visit. The house felt filled with love. Pictures of her and her son were proudly displayed, along with beautiful and happy furnishings. The best makeover was Glennis herself, but it had nothing to do with her hair or makeup – it was her spirit that was filled with laugher and hope.

Hell and Back

The small white cross stood on the side of the road, just a few feet after Tall Tree Lane. The name etched into the wooden memorial read Shiloh.

Crosses, memorials, and death shrines often mark the death spot due to an accident. The deceased's name or initials are inscribed on the markers, sometimes surrounded by flowers, stuffed animals, or another memento. It is a significant statement of grief, love, and remembrance.

Years ago the deceased would be buried where they fell, making it their final place of rest. Although that's not today's tradition, the sentiment remains with a tribute. We often see it with celebrity deaths, from Princess Diana to Prince.

There are thoughts that the tradition may have begun from a Spanish tradition. During the funeral, the pallbearers would carry the casket from the church to the cemetery. Each time the casket had to be set down for the carriers to rest, a stone would be set upon the route. The journey would continue until they reached the final resting destination. And each and every time a stone was set where the casket laid in wait, it was a reminder to stop and pray. It was a reminder to remember that life is short, that life is heavy.

Whether a dusty country road or a busy highway, you've likely seen a cross, wilted flowers, or rain-stained stuffed animals denoting a shrine for someone's departed loved one. Maybe you've wondered about the story behind it, said a prayer, or maybe you simply looked away.

I love wandering the cemeteries, and some may find it macabre, but each cemetery is its own museum with stones and sculptures of grave art.

I was researching local cemeteries for a local news story and taking photographs of various historical haunts. One cemetery I ventured to sat on a hill in the middle of a local Michigan suburb. Dating back to the mid-1700s, I was intrigued by the stonework and various stories left behind with each epitaph. As I stood admiring a statue of a weeping angel that sat atop a large stone I felt a tap on my shoulder.

Whether I'm investigating the paranormal or I'm visiting a cemetery I make it a practice to protect myself from anything negative.

It doesn't mean that negative can't attempt communication but it lessens the possibility.

I turned to see a spirit of a man wearing a large black hat. He looked somber.

"See that grave there, that's mine. I need your help."

I walked to the gravesite he had pointed at to see. There stood an upright plain grave marker with just his name and birth and death dates—Humphrey Marshall Delaney, b. 1792 d. Nov. 15, 1836. Wrapped around the marker was barbed wire, rusted and tied tight.

"I need you to cut that," he said.

It was something I'd never seen before, and there was no way I was changing a grave site.

"Why's it there?" I asked, looking suspiciously at Humphrey. My radar was going off telling me to not trust the Abraham Lincoln doppelganger.

"Not sure, really, but it's keeping me from crossing. It's been a long time from the looks of it," he said sadly, shrugging his shoulders.

That it has, I thought, but for him to not find a light or an ability to cross was odd. I tried to see a light on the other side for him to help walk him into but there was nothing there.

It was as if he was bound to the earth.

I could smell sulfur in the air. To many paranormal enthusiasts, this is a sign of a demonic presence, based on the theory that hell is a physical place, deep within the core of the earth. The further you dig, the more sulfuric it becomes. Therefore, the smell of sulfur is thought to be the calling card of hell, Satan, and demons.

I took it as my sign to leave. Demanding that Humphrey stays put, that he wasn't allowed to follow, I headed to the local historical society to see if I might be able to discover the secret of Humphrey.

"Kristy, it's so weird that you're here today. This lady called, her name's Jeanette. She just moved into a new house down the road from the cemetery, oddly enough, and she thinks she's being haunted," Michelle, the supervisor of the historical society, told me.

"Haunted how?" I received hundreds of *I'm haunted* emails and calls a month and have determined that most paranormal activity is mice in the attic, bees in the wall, bad plumbing, or a heaven hello from a family member on the other side. It's sad to say, but I've grown skeptical, and maybe a bit cynical, of haunted reports.

"She's frightened, and Kristy, I don't think this lady scares easily. She's tough as bullets. She reports she's been pushed going down her stairs numerous times. She's awoken to a dark shadow, a man with a hat on, standing over her, and then there's…"

Before I let her finish I held up my hand. "Stop. A man with a hat? Like an old stovepipe hat?"

"Yes, exactly! Also, her husband just died, so there's that going on. And from what I understand," Michelle said, "it didn't sound like he was a good guy."

I grabbed Jeanette' number and address from Michelle and went to leave, almost forgetting to ask her about Humphrey.

Michelle turned white as a ghost when I asked her. "Have you ever seen that marker on the side of Haggerts Road? People often leave toys or flowers there? Humphrey killed an entire family in 1836: the wife, husband, and their five children, all because they

were making too much noise. He was working the night shift, trying to sleep during the day, and between five kids, their poultry, and
their dogs, he was disturbed. So he took an axe and murdered them
while they slept, then burned down the house. The marker on the
side of the road is near where their house sat. It didn't take any
deep detective work to discover who did it. The blood stains led
them next door to his home, which I believe is … the land that Jeanette bought," Michelle added, looking horrified as the pieces fit
together.

"Obviously not the same house, but the same land?"

"Right. The town burned down his house with him in it. Then
they buried his body in the grave, wrapping a barbed wire around
the tombstone that his mother bought for him. The town wanted
an unmarked grave, but his family were good citizens. It wasn't
their fault their son was a crazy man."

"Barbed wire?"

"It was a binding ceremony, binding his soul to the earth to
serve out his eternal damnation."

Something about it didn't sit well with me, but I called Jeanette
while sitting in the historical society office to see when we could
meet. She asked if I could come right then.

Her delicate skin and light hair and features were shrouded by
the fear that hung on her shoulders like a shawl.

I knew I had to tell her the history of her property, but I didn't
believe it would require her to move. We just needed to find a release so that she could move on and not get caught up in the energy of the past. Possibly her past, possibly the property's past and
Humphrey's past, and possibly a combination.

"How do we do that?" she asked me, her frail body quaking.

I could see the spirit of her husband standing there, and although he wasn't a violent soul like Humphrey was, he set out to hurt others without apology or regret. Standing next to him was Humphrey. It was as if they were both tag teaming to absorb Jeanette' good energy to feed their own in-between existence.

"We cross them."

"Will they go?" she asked unconvinced.

"We will call on helpers," I reassured her.

We did just that. Sitting in her quaint living room, with her vintage radio singing out jazz music, we held hands and called on assistance from the other side to take the earthly prisoners to transfer them to the next life, cutting the cords off of them from this lifetime. They resisted, and fought back, unsure of where their destination would be, but within an hour the energy felt like sunshine at the beach and even Jeanette had removed her soul shawl, a newfound freedom.

"Why me?" she asked. "I get the property location, but it's been here for a hundred plus years and my realtor said the family I bought it from loved this home for over thirty years!" Standing up and stretching, she walked up and picked up a picture of her late husband. "Am I that bad of a person?"

"That's just it. You're that *good* of a person who's had bad things happen."

With her grief, depression, and life changes, she made herself open to the low vibrations of energies and they weren't just binding themselves to earth, but to her. I'm not certain that Frederick or Humphrey went to hell, I believe that the case more than likely was they were bound to the in-between where they were damaging those who deserved their happily ever now.

Cutting Cords

Our thoughts, feelings, words, and actions are all forms of energy, and everything we think, feel, say, or do create a reality for the now and set precedence for the future. We are each responsible for everything that happens in our life. It's a hard nugget to swallow. Those who are miserable or negative often want to blame everyone else. Those going through a tough time often want to be the victim in order to support their misery. The Law of Attraction teaches us, though, that miserable people will continue to find misery, and happy people will find happiness because it's a song that is sung, magnetizing more of what is the same. If you can't seem to find your vibration or song due to life situations, sometimes a cord cutting has to be done. It doesn't necessarily mean that you lose people in your life that aren't on your wave length, but you will discover that they may not enjoy your vibration and step aside.

Jeanette never had any more paranormal activity after that day, and I left the binding on Humphrey's gravestone.

Every time I drive by the road side memorial I still say a prayer for everyone, sending good thoughts for a fair afterlife for everyone involved.

With every person we interact with we attach cords from them back to ourself. If the relationship is unhealthy, however, it often anchors us to unhealthy and negative patterns that can drain our psychic and emotional energy. Even connections filled with love can be draining and create stagnation.

Energy can revive us, or drain us, and one thing that can work is something called Cord Cutting. It is like smudging for the soul where you release the energy, people, or situations that aren't lighting your soul up. Let's be honest, though, letting go isn't easy. Saying no is hard. And standing your ground and speaking your truth isn't always well received. So many of us spend our lives sacrificing our own happiness in order to avoid confrontations. Most of us know we can't fix anyone, but we still keep allowing our inner magic to be stolen. It might be from our past, or our now. You don't plant a garden without tilling beforehand, why would you think that you can bring in love, light, happiness, and positivity with the weeds of yesterdays?

If you are feeling drained, it may be because you have cords wrapped around you and you need to make space to bring in happiness. A cord cutting doesn't require a light worker to do it; you are your best light worker. It doesn't remove the love or memory; it simply cleans up the residue that is stealing your sunshine.

Cord Cutting Meditation

To cut your own cords through meditation, begin by calling on Archangel Michael. Take some time to relax your body and relax your mind. The more you are unaware of your body during this time, the easier it is for you to concentrate with your mind on just relaxing.

Take a deep breath, hold it for a moment, and slowly let it out. Allow all your tension to leave your body. With each breath out you release, and with each breath in you take in joy, hope, love, and peace.

Imagine with every breath a very large, white ball of light moving toward you, closer and closer, getting larger and larger, and surrounding every part of you like walking into a cloud. It relaxes you from the tips of your toes to the top of your head, encouraging you to release, relax, and let go of what isn't serving you in this lifetime or other lifetimes.

"I accept this white light as my armor."

Now surrounded by white light, your constant protector, call any other angels, guides, or ascended masters to help release any lower-energy experiences.

"I call on my angels to help disconnect and release lower energies from the past and present."

Envision Archangel Michael's blue sword and grab ahold of it. With his guidance, envision the emotional cords that are binding you to lower energies. You can even call on them such as—I cut through my grief; I cut through the hurt of the divorce; I cut through my sense of failure and so on. You can also cut through the cords that attach you to people or places that are not serving you any longer, zapping your strength. It is important that while you do this, you forgive yourself for being a part of the experiences and see that there are lessons, not just scars associated with it. The longer you have been attached, the thicker the cord is to cut.

Once you've cut your cords, ask Archangel Michael to seal each cord end with love and peace to reduce the chances of the cords reconnecting.

Offer a prayer of gratitude and know that it took a long time to connect those negative cords and you may need to do it several times. The more cords you have wrapped around you, the less likely the chance you have in feeling centered or placed on the right path. After doing the exercise, it is important to drink a bunch of water to detoxify. You may also want to do this while getting a massage or reflexology (just make sure to tell them what you are doing, in case you start to cry).

Chapter Eleven
What the Hell

We all know a person who lives within their misery. It's too sunny. It's too rainy. You're too happy. Or too sad. I once was written up by a supervisor for being too positive and happy before nine in the morning and his first cup of coffee. It stayed put in my employee folder and was mentioned on my evaluation. To him every essence of happy was hell. I sorely wanted to get out of that work situation because it was slowly changing me into someone I didn't like— miserable. Then my guides told me to send those who are living in their hell as much love as I could. Not only would it hopefully help them, it would also protect against holes in the aura that darkness could ooze through, like a roach infested hotel. One sneaks into your suitcase and then invades your own home. Hell on earth can do the same.

Till Death Do Us Part

The middle-aged man stood in spirit next to me. His frustration was apparent by his pacing. The room of a dozen women stared at me as I tried to keep graceful.

"Tell her I'm her husband. How could she forget about me?" he balked.

"He says he's your husband. And he is bald. Was bald even before his cancer treatments," I added.

"Tell her I'm Rich. I'm her husband," he kept repeating.

I rarely got names. Well, I got names but I doubted the names, though at this point I had nothing to lose.

"He says that his name is Rich."

The women looked at me, still shaking her head no.

"I have a grandfather that passed from cancer, and he was bald," a lady in the group chimed in.

I would never make it fit, and Rich was bound and determined that this lady with the large floral purse sitting on her lap was his wife.

Taking a deep breathe I decided to move on.

"I don't have your grandpa," I told the young lady, "I do have your dad. He passed from…" and I continued to give readings to everyone in the group all the while noticing that not-Rich's wife was getting more and more agitated.

"I rarely do this," I told the lady with the big floral purse, "but can I ask who you are looking for?"

The lady wiped her eyes with the tissue that she held for the whole hour and nodded. "Yes, I'm looking for Richard, my husband."

The women in the room all inhaled.

"And he passed from cancer?" I asked.

"Yes."

"And was he bald even before his treatments."

"He had no treatments, but yes, he was bald."

I squinted at her, wondering where she was, or I was, an hour before when I brought through the exact same information.

"Do you have a name that is sort of like a male's name?"

She nodded and shared that her name was Miles.

Richard had stopped pacing and was eerily staring at his wife. His soul, hollow.

"Do you feel that he's haunting you?" I asked, putting my hand on her shoulder in support. It was met by a mess of tears.

Miles shared her story of marital abuse with the group of strangers, and then her discoveries after Richard's death. "I finally thought I had my escape," she cried, "but as soon as we moved into the new home the haunting began.

She went to a local psychic shop and got white sage. Following the instructions, she smudged the home, but it just seemed to spur more activity.

"Did you happen to go out on a date?"

Miles turned wide eyed at me and nodded in shame. Richard was making sure he kept a hold of her even from the afterlife.

"Is he in heaven? If he's in heaven how can he haunt me so?" she pondered, playing with her purse straps.

I didn't feel that Richard was in heaven at all, and with the void I felt around his soul, I felt like I needed more information and we arranged that I come to her home the very next day.

Pulling into the driveway of the old white farmhouse you could feel the veil of darkness, even though the sun shone. Miles met me in the driveway, and taking my hand she led me up the chipped cement steps and into the living room. The walls were shrugging off the blue damask patterned wallpaper and the ceiling was crying plaster everywhere.

"I know it's a mess," confirming that I had the worst poker face, "but I see potential. I'm going to paint and fix all this. In fact, I already tore out the kitchen cabinets and the tile flooring. Here, come see," she led me into a large but awkward shaped kitchen. An old wooden screen door let in the breeze and I could almost see kids from the past running in and out while their mom yelled to stop slamming the door, and choose in or out.

"What's that?" I asked pointing to the large red stain in the middle of the kitchen, praying she was going to say paint.

"I discovered it after I pulled the tile up. And then I did some research."

I cringed, all the while knowing she wasn't going to say that someone had spilled a lot of paint. In 1910, just a year after the home was built, immigrants from France, Max and Ada, had a volatile marriage.

"You see how far my closest neighbor is? Apparently the arguing was daily and echoed over to them. It was one evening in November, the neighbor was feeding his chickens when he heard the shot gun ring out, and then he heard another. Max and Ada both lay here in the kitchen, stove still on with fresh pressed coffee and homemade biscuits in the oven. Their children watched from the back stairs there," Miles pointed to a plain stairway that I hadn't even noticed. "The next owner put down the tile that I just pulled up."

There were quite a few layers to Miles' issue, but before I could ask my next question it was as if someone turned the thermostat on as high as it could, and we both began fanning ourselves.

"Wait," Miles whispered. "Now the radio will come on." Sure enough, the radio in the living room began to sing. "That's Skip Davis: 'Ghost Got My Woman.'"

"Wait, what?"

"I had to look it up. I had no idea who it was."

I certainly had no clue either, but we took a few minutes to listen. Unsettling, angry, and haunting, the singer crooned.

Before the song was over, I saw her husband on the front stairway, a stairway much more elegant than the back one.

"The river is thick with fire, and I can't breathe there," he told me.

"Hell? Are you describing hell?"

"There are no birds, or breeze. There's no love, just hate. I practiced evil here, I'm damned to create evil there. I'm in the house of the wicked, the realm of the dead. I am the beast, just as you can choose to be the beast too."

I shuddered in the heat as Miles stared on at me.

"He's here, isn't he? I knew it was him who wants to still have a hold on me."

"We are given keys, Miles. Upon our birth, we are given keys and these keys unlock whatever doors we want to unlock. Your husband unlocked the doors of darkness and pulled you in with him. It's time for you to throw those keys away."

"So do I have to move?" Miles, asked confused, thinking I was being literal.

"No. You have to release Richard. It's like he's feeding on you and your weakness. Just like he hid so much, you too hid your trueness from him."

Although we were indoors, and it was April and mild out, the room became uncannily windy.

"I release my chains," Miles shouted through the wind tunnel. "I'm no longer connected to you, Richard, or any darkness, and I shine light into my soul, and around me and all that is mine. I send you out to the sea of your own judgment. Be gone."

The temperature immediately lowered and the wind stopped. Miles fell to her knees, giving up all her strength.

"He's gone?" She looked up at me.

I nodded, bent down on the floor, and helped her up on the couch, her legs still wobbling.

Miles ended up staying in the house for another year, remodeling it to something out of a home magazine, and then sold it. The history of the home she purchased helped to feed the already negative energy attached to her and kept open the portal of darkness. Although she closed off most of the doorways, no matter what we did we couldn't seem to close them all off. The home sold quickly, despite Miles being very forthcoming with the 1910 history. The radio still comes on once in a while, the new homeowners informed her, but otherwise all is peaceful.

It's Always Monday in Hell

Liam hated Fridays, Saturdays, and Sundays, and he hated Mondays just the same.

While most loved the weekend, they required Liam to be the husband and father that he found out thirteen years too late that he didn't want. But the last weekend was different, he told himself as he drove into work Monday morning. Or at least it will be different; he told his wife that he wanted a divorce. She could have anything she wanted, even their three kids, he just wanted out. Did he have another woman, his wife cried? Nope, not another woman. Heck, not even another man. He just wanted out. He didn't want to worry about anyone telling him to pick this or that up after work. Or that it was the wrong this or that. He didn't want to answer to anyone as to where he was, even though he didn't go anywhere, but he might if he didn't have anyone to answer to. No, he simply wanted peace and solitude.

What will she tell the kids, his wife screamed? Tell them I'm dead, he told her before leaving the house that Monday for the daily grind as a computer specialist for a leading supply chain company where he went to his office, coded, met with people, coded, and went home to a house he hated, to a wife he hated, and to kids he hated. He'd choose his work over all that. She made him feel dead he told himself every morning, afternoon, and night, and there was no use pretending anymore. Oh, his wife and kids weren't horrible people. In fact, he did love his wife when they first met, and he was happy when the kids were born, but something changed inside of him. His mother tried to tell him it was a mid-life crisis and that a sport's car or maybe an affair would fix it. Yes, his mother told him to have an affair. Nobody could understand because he, himself, didn't understand. He wasn't depressed, he would say, he simply didn't care. He was numb. Scary numb. And he believed he'd be happy if he lived his anesthetic life without having to deal with senseless emotions or answering to anyone.

He drove to work with robotic movement. The same road. The same scenery. The same coffee and bagel. It was all the same. For now.

It was November 11th, Veterans Day, and traffic was lighter than normal. Whether for the day or for the weather, he wasn't sure. An abnormally early winter had pounded the area in late October and Mother Nature wasn't about to let up. The roads were slushy and wet, but he had an all-wheel drive vehicle, so he refused to go slower than the speed limit, passing cars here and there along the way.

"Stupid drivers," he yelled. "It's as if you've never seen snow! Don't like it, get off the road. Get off *my* road, and stay home."

He pulled on his wheel to make another pass, but the slush on the side of the fast lane seemed to pull his wheels into it and no matter how much overcorrecting he did with the steering wheel, he continued to slide. Attempting to brake, the ice underneath him was unforgiving and he slid down the embankment, flipping the car several times before smashing into a large pine tree.

The airbags deployed, but luckily the car landed right side up and he was able to open the door and step outside. It was then that he realized that not everything was okay. Looking inside the car was his physical body, bloodied and distorted. Confused, he watched as people ran down the snowy causeway to help get him out, but he was right there standing in the cold. No matter how much he attempted to get their attention nobody was listening.

The first responders came and he saw the one man shake his head at his partner after checking for a pulse.

"Hello?" he screamed. "Are you an idiot too? I'm right here. My wife needs to know ..."

Liam stopped to contemplate what he said, leveraging all that he'd done. When he saw them put his body into a black body bag and rush off, he knew he was dead. If he ever wanted to be alone, he realized that his wish had been granted, but at what cost?

He didn't know if he wandered around for hours or days, but he did find his way to his own funeral. Liam was sensible and had a large life insurance policy. At least he was good for something for Kate and the kids, he thought. His mom wept while his wife sat in the front row, staring, no tears. Numb. Possibly even relieved.

I thought there was supposed to be a white light or something, he thought to himself. And that my dad would meet me. Or grandma. Or angels. Or someone. But there was nobody meeting him and no comforting white light to help guide him to the other side.

Maybe this is hell? Liam wondered.

———

Several years ago Liam found me.

I was going through a trying time, my vibration lower than it should've been. I was being called to help on some darker paranormal cases and I was leaving myself vulnerable to the lower vibrational spirits. I knew what I was doing, but I wanted to help these people, and there was possibly an ego involved. All the while I was putting myself and my family at risk. I'd lived the scary experiences as a child and so when the shadows began to pace in the hallway outside my kid's bedroom door, as if waiting to pounce, I knew I had to seal off the doorway of hell and the in-between. My job as a mother wasn't to bring the wolves into the house, it was to scare them away. I was trying to balance my paranormal priorities when Liam crept in.

My kids, Connor and Micaela, had just finished school for the year, and the next morning we were packing for a trip out east. Chuck's kids decided they were too old for a family vacation, with responsibilities of jobs and boyfriends, so they stayed back in Michigan while we made the long drive to Plymouth, Massachusetts. A week away in a quaint home with ocean front views, so much to explore, and side trips to Boston and Salem, we were hoping for a magical time.

It was after a visit to a local Bostonian cemetery when Liam appeared.

"So you have unfinished business?" I asked him, sitting out on the deck with the dark clouds casting shadows.

It was only three p.m., but being by the water wasn't energizing any of us; instead, all we wanted to do was sleep. The unseasonably cold temperatures and gray skies weren't helping either, and the kids were not enjoying the vacation at all, begging to just go home. We were two days in with another five days to go. Personally, I wanted to go home too.

"I just want my heaven," he demanded, sounding like a child who got the wrong color gumball. "I earned it, after all."

When you die you decide that you deserve a form of punishment or a form of paradise. There are bags you carry that are real, true, and not simply creations of your mind. It's hard to walk into the light when you are so afraid of judgement, so the bags of regret and resentment fill up and are dragged behind. Resistance is futile when the truth can't be hidden away. Your own worst enemy is truly yourself, but you have to face that enemy. Liam didn't seem to want to face the true enemy.

"You don't earn heaven, you create heaven," I lectured. "How long have you been gone?"

Tapping his foot in impatience, he glared at me. "It seems I've found another person who pretends who can help, but can't or just won't," Liam snorted.

I was about to match Liam's presumptuous attitude but realized that was what got me in this situation in the first place, attracting his spirit. My low vibration was a match for his, and I needed to see his arrogance and raise my altitude on my attitude. I most certainly wanted to help, but he wasn't going to bully me into it.

"You are in hell because you've created it." I simply told him. "You have the opportunity to forgive yourself for everything you've done, but it's too late to receive forgiveness of your loved ones. What's done is done, you can't fix it with them and I have a feeling you don't realize anything was broken to begin with."

Liam's arrogance put him in a perpetual corner where he was simply running into the same wall over and over, wanting someone to pull him out. Even if that happened, he would simply go back to run into the same wall and call it that person's fault.

There was no fixing what already was, but we each have an opportunity to make changes in our life every single day. Unfortunately, most believe that they'll have tomorrow, and tomorrow is never guaranteed.

I couldn't help Liam, but he did help me remind myself to stop my self-wallowing for situations not under my control.

We made the most of the trip, staying the duration of the week. When we got home, though, every one of us found more appreciation for home. I decided to put my pout and self-pity away and be grateful instead. There are so many things to be grateful for, but isn't it funny that when one (or two or three or ...) things go wrong that we forget about all the good? There are many out there who tend to destroy the positive because they can't see the sunshine in their own lives—well keep your storm clouds to yourself, and if I want to shine, damn it, I am going to shine and shine bright!

Unfortunately, I don't think Liam ever found his true home and is still wandering around in his eternal gloom.

The Devil Within

Leslie Ray Charping died in January 2017 after losing his battle with cancer, leaving the earth "29 years longer than expected and much longer than he deserved," read the obituary, which ran on the Carnes Funeral Home website.

Leslie Ray "Popeye" Charping was born in Galveston, Texas on November 20, 1942 and passed away January 30, 2017, which was 29 years longer than expected and much longer than he deserved. Leslie battled with cancer in his latter years and lost his battle, ultimately due to being the horses ass he was known for. He leaves behind 2 relieved children; a son Leslie Roy Charping and daughter, Sheila Smith along with six grandchildren and countless other victims including an ex-wife, relatives, friends, neighbors, doctors, nurses and random strangers.

At a young age, Leslie quickly became a model example of bad parenting combined with mental illness and a complete commitment to drinking, drugs, womanizing and be-ing generally offensive. Leslie enlisted to serve in the Navy, but not so much in a brave & patriotic way but more as part of a plea deal to escape sentencing on criminal charges. While enlisted, Leslie was the Navy boxing champion and went on to sufficiently embarrass his family and country by spending the remainder of his service in the Balboa Mental Health Hospital receiving much needed mental healthcare services.

Leslie was surprisingly intelligent, however he lacked ambition and motivation to do anything more than being reckless, wasteful, squandering the family savings and fan-tasizing about get rich quick schemes. Leslie's hobbies in-cluded being abusive to his family, expediting trips to heaven for the beloved family pets and fishing, which he was less skilled with than the previously mentioned. Leslie's life served no other obvious purpose, he did not contribute to society or serve his community and he possessed no re-deeming qualities besides quick whited sarcasm which was amusing during his sober days.

With Leslie's passing he will be missed only for what he never did; being a loving husband, father and good friend. No services will be held, there will be no prayers for eternal peace and no apologizes to the family he tortured. Leslie's remains will be cremated and kept in the barn until "Ray," the family donkey's wood shavings run out. Leslie's passing proves that evil does in fact die and hopefully marks a time of healing and safety for all.

Critical obituaries aren't rare. When Edgar Allan Poe died, Rufus Griswold anonymously penned Poe's obituary using the signature of "Ludwig." Appearing in the evening edition of the *New York Tribune* on October 9, 1849.

> Edgar Allan Poe is dead. He died in Baltimore the day before yesterday. This announcement will startle many, but few will be grieved by it. The poet was well known, personally or by reputation, in all this country; he had readers in England, and in several states of Continental Europe; but he had few or no friends; and the regrets for his death will be suggested principally by the consideration that in him literary art lost one of its most brilliant but erratic stars.

The lynch mob of judgement continues into the afterlife. With the stop of a heartbeat, the effects of abuse, lies, and past personal quarrels linger like low storm clouds that threaten severe weather.

"I could've written that same obituary for my own mother," Terri told me, and took back her phone after having me read the news story.

She wrapped a blanket around her long lean legs, shivering, although my office was set at seventy-two degrees. In her early sixties, Terri's vulnerable soul still ached for a mother's love that she never got, and never would.

"When we got the diagnosis of her cancer, my siblings and I celebrated," she said playing with the pills on the green afghan. Feeling the weight of my look, she looked up at me. "I know it sounds horrible, but so was our childhood. I wish I'd stood up for myself then like I do now."

I wasn't excusing her mother's behavior or history, but I was disturbed at how the abuse still pooled around her like stagnant waters.

"Perhaps you wouldn't be as strong as you are now if it wasn't for the battles you faced before."

"When you were a kid, did your parents ever give you the pop cans to take back for extra money?" Before I could answer Terri continued. "Mom would go one step further and have us go to the neighbor's house and ask for their pop cans, telling us to tell them we were collecting money for this or that charity, only for her to take the money to buy booze." Terri shrugged off the blanket and carefully folded it, taking a moment to think. In a low tone she started again. "Not only did she lie, but she forced us to lie. I'm worried she helped seal our own damnation. We lived a life of hell with her. How do I know I won't live my afterlife with her too?"

"I was the devil himself, or herself," Terri's mother simply stated, standing there in spirit, overhearing my session with her daughter. "It's true. She's using the mildest of examples of what a horrific person I was," she confessed.

Terri's mother was spending her afterlife in a continuous loop, reliving the pain and hurt she caused everyone that ever met her. Booze was her demon; lying, her devil; and she was in her own hell. Nobody needed to send her there, though, or wish it upon her. It was a judgment that would happen regardless of wishing.

Terri's wish of karma wasn't hurting her mother, it was hurting her. When you wish bad karma on others, it comes back on you like a boomerang. We don't get what we deserve in life or the afterlife; we get what we attract, sow, and then reap. Revengeful thinking clips on your soul like a magnet asking for more of the same.

Karma will happen, but not on our timeline and not from our wanting.

"I can't uncreate what your mother did to you, Terri," I said softly. "I'm so sorry for everything she did. She knows that now. Heck, I think she knew that then but was so consumed in her own pain she didn't realize she was spewing that on you all. No excuses from her or from me; I'm just explaining."

"She used to call me fat. She said nobody would ever want a fatty, and that became my nickname. My sisters and brother had their own horrific nicknames too and we started to live up to them. I continued to gain weight and then I began to drink away the sound of my mom's voice."

"You lived in a hell, but you have the opportunity to pull yourself out and not see yourself there anymore, here or when your physical body transitions."

Terri rubbed her chin in thought. "I don't want the hell anymore, Kristy. I don't want her to drag me down anymore."

One Word

The power of words, even just one, is incredible. In today's world where we have the tools to express ourselves in so many different forums, our words can be inspirational or hurtful. They reach a broad audience and spread messages of peace and sometimes hate. We can support someone from across the world, or tear down a complete stranger in the matter of a moment.

One family I met with lost their daughter to two words. *Kill yourself.*

That was the two words a thirteen-year-old girl was texted two hours before her parents found her lifeless body in her bedroom, surrounded by her stuffed animals. They had no idea that Samantha was being bullied by several classmates all because she got braces.

It started with a girl telling her that she was ugly with her braces and she should kill herself. It wasn't just one time, it was several times—over and over and over and over, and she began to believe it. She was thirteen years old, sensitive, shy, quiet, respectful, and beautiful, but she was being torn down and ripped to pieces.

Most believe it could never happen to them. Never believe that a word, or words, could make someone so depressed that they would take drastic measures. Remember back to the time you felt upset with someone. Wasn't it words that were used to hurt you? Words can be, and are, a deadly weapon. But they can also be the most beautiful things ever.

The internet has given many people an unwritten right to act as judge and jury, and they can be cruel while doing it, but we have to be realistic—there's nothing we can do about it.

We can step back from the sword so it doesn't stab, realizing that there's no fight, with you or them, if you get out of the way. Not everyone is that strong, though.

Words can cause harm, but there will come a time where you are smack dab in the battle of words; it's just going to happen and you can't stop it. You can, however, find ways to let it go, and help teach and support others, especially kids, on ways to diffuse the hurtful words. Because haters are going to hate and words are going to hurt, but you don't have to make their hell your hell.

Terri's mother put herself in helix of damnation that neither Terri nor her siblings needed to wish upon her. If you've experienced your own hellish life, it's time to release the weight of hardship. You've been carrying it around for much too long. We're all a work in progress, but that doesn't mean that the hell state of mind should be carried over to the afterlife.

Everybody has a past, but you have the opportunity to leave it in the past or carry it with you into the now, into the future, and into the ever after. You have to create your life and you create your hell as much as you can create your heaven. You have to believe it can happen and you have to hustle for it. Not everybody can accomplish what you can accomplish—and that is what makes you so special. Life is scarier holding on to the shadows than walking into the sunshine. There will always be defeats, but it takes moxie to not allow those defeats to make you feel defeated.

Sometimes we have to hit rock bottom in order to rebuild. Everyone in this lifetime has the ability to patch, and patch, and tear it off, and start again. There is a certain pride that sometimes makes us keep repairing, but it takes an even bigger person to ask for help, with better tools and a better team surrounding us.

Unfortunately, I've seen too many living this existence in their personal hell in hopes of it being better in their after, but how can you create something for later if you don't work for the vision of it now? Everyone has an immortal spirit with conscious thoughts to create their afterlife. I closed my doorway to hell several years back, no longer interested in communing with the banished. In life I'd rather spend time with those joyful and who are at peace or who want peace. In the afterlife I hope to do the same.

Chapter Twelve

In Between

Some have called what I refer to as "the in-between" as purgatory. Others call it "the left behind," while many consider it a spiritual jail; and then there are some who believe it to be a healing room. It's like waiting your turn for major surgery and then once you have the surgery you have to go into recovery, and you have to be patient during that healing. But first you have to allow the healing to happen, releasing the residue of sin.

Dryhthelm, a monk associated with the Historia Eccelesistica gentis Anglorum of Bede in from c 700, caught a glimpse of the afterlife after a brief illness. Dryhthelm died and came back to tell his experience of his tour of heaven, hell, and purgatory. He was not allowed to view what he described as a place called Paradise, more beautiful and filled with more light than even heaven. He described purgatory as a place of extreme heat and cold, hell as a place where souls burn, and heaven as a place of intense light. Purgatory, as he experienced it, was a staging post, a middle for heaven and hell. It was a place that reminded you of who you were and then offered you a choice of how you wanted to dedicate your life.

We all have regrets in life, and when the physical body and this life ends, those regrets can stay firmly planted.

Often we think of purgatory for those who've committed suicide, but that's not a hard and fast rule. I've encountered spirits of those who took their own life who are happy and in heaven and then on the other side of the coin I've encountered spirits who have lingered, refusing to move on because of their intense guilt.

That is most often reason why the soul doesn't go into the light and stays stagnant in the in-between—because the soul feels some sort of shame, guilt, or fear. Other times it is a family member that is so distraught that they use their own energy to bind the soul to earth.

Others realize they made mistakes, and so desperately try to find their bodies, their family, and re-connect with their life. Sometimes they stay in wait to cross with their family members. And others feel that they can help more by staying in the in-between than if they were to cross over. Those who linger aren't alone in the in-between. There are angels and others who try to help guide them to their forever.

Barbara's twin brother and best friend had tragically passed away in a work accident. They say that twins have a connection, and Barb and Blake didn't disappoint with that theory. Before Barb got married, Blake's wife sat down with Barb's fiancé to explain that he couldn't get jealous of the twins' relationship. It was special and it was something neither of them would ever understand, so there's no use in trying. They had a bond that extended outside of the uterus. So when Barb received the phone call that Blake had died, she already knew. She felt his soul's departure from his body, as if pieces of her own soul were being smashed into a million pieces. She sat on the floor in the work bathroom and sobbed. Her co-worker and friend looked everywhere to tell her the news, when she found her.

"Blake's dead. I feel it," Barb told her coworker. "He's dead."

She was right. Details were still sketchy, but Blake had been working at a construction site when he was thrown from an excavator and run over, passing immediately.

There was no comforting her. There was no peace in knowing he was in a better place, or in anything else everyone was trying to convince her of. He wasn't in peace if he was without her, and vice versa. Instead of going to the funeral lunch, Barb headed to the local bar and began drinking heavily. Not a drinker, other than casual, it didn't take her long to start seeing sideways, and after the sixth drink she was close to passed out.

"Someone needs to call her a cab," a patron yelled to the bartender, horrified that she was served so much.

The bartender reached for the phone, but one man stood up at a table where he was eating lunch with another, both dressed in uniforms, and he said he'd just drive her. He knew who she was and where she lived.

"C'mon Barb. It's time to go home," the stranger said, helping her up and out the door to his car. The other man opened the door and helped her into the passenger seat, taking a seat in the back.

She only lived a few miles away, and sure enough the man knew exactly where she lived. Took her keys, opened the door and set her on the couch.

"I'm sorry, Barb. I have to go, but I love you. Stop being stupid," he told her before leaving.

When she woke up from her drunken stupor and realized what happened, she sobered up quickly and raced to the bar. This time to ask questions, not for another drink.

"I'm not sure who it was," the bartender said. "He comes in once a week for lunch. He always wears a uniform with SGE on it, so I assume he's on a work break. Maybe check there."

She didn't have to check there. It was her brother who drove her home, she knew that.

"The man in the back of the car, though, Kristy? Who was that?"

It was his guide or his angel, probably helping him with one more connection before assisting him to the other side.

"Tell him I'll stop being stupid," Barb joked. "He just better find a way to visit once he makes his journey."

"Oh, he will. That connection doesn't stop into the afterlife. He just won't be able to drive you anyplace more than likely," I laughed.

Peace Out

Orson always felt different. He wasn't as smart as his peers, and his parents sometimes whispered that they feared he was autistic or that he might have Asperger's. It made him feel like he didn't measure up in some ways. Although his parents were good to him and loved him, learning was hard and frustrating.

Both of his parents, Christine and Dale, were Ivy League alumni, started a multimillion dollar business upon graduation, and rubbed elbows with the elite. When Christine became pregnant, Dale wasn't exactly happy. He didn't want their jet-setting days and cocktail party nights to disappear, but when Orson was born and he held that small bundle, all the materialistic things that he found important immediately became void. Dale's family was surprised, but thrilled. Christine thought they should hire a night-time nanny, but Dale would have none of it. He had no problem getting up in the middle of the night to feed and hold Orson, letting Christine sleep in. Over his morning coffee, he would read the newspaper out loud to Orson, as if he could understand. His assistant would often find Dale napping in his office during noon, and she just left him. The baby changed the way he dealt with his staff, he was softer and kinder. And their business boomed in return. It's as if he let go of the control he tried so hard to hold on to, and the flow of prosperity was his gift.

When Orson first began school, the teaching staff suggested that Orson receive some testing and some extra help, but his parents would have none of it. Now at ten years old, they regretted not following through on that earlier rather than later and wondered what to do next.

Neither Christine nor Dale ever judged or ridiculed their child, it was always unconditional love. They just worried about his future, knowing they wouldn't be around forever. They wanted him to have a happy future, but they also didn't want to hand everything to him.

Some days being a patient parent was easier than others. Orson had been whining about studying for the past week, and Christine and Dale were having financial issues with their company after a botched merger, and everyone was on edge. When Orson brought home a D+ on the science test he'd been shuffling his feet on studying for, Dale regrettably let him have it.

"Are you stupid? I didn't raise a stupid kid, Orson. I'm tired of you taking the easy way, and things will have to change starting now. Go to your room. I don't even want to see you until dinner."

Christine tried to intervene, but Dale gave her the look to back off. As Orson raced to his room, Christine started dinner, wanting so badly to go comfort Orson. She called her mom while she cut the vegetables for the salad. "Maybe Dale's right, though, Mom. Maybe we've babied him for too long. But honestly, this is just one test. We've all been stressed out."

After hanging up the phone, she put the salads on the dining table and called for Dale and Orson. Dale came to the table, his eyes swollen. He pretended to be tough, but he was a softie.

"Where's Orson?" he asked "I went to his room to apologize and figured you told him to help you in the kitchen."

Immediately Christine began to panic. It wasn't like Orson to not be in his room. They both raced around their home, opening closet doors even to see if he was hiding. It was then that Dale discovered the door to his gun safe open.

Orson's body was found an hour later by Christine. He shot himself down by the creek in back of the house. There wasn't a note, a goodbye, nothing. Life stopped in that moment for Orson, and hell began for Christine and Dale.

Suicide isn't a one-way pass to hell like many believe. Often when someone takes their life their loved ones are angry, confused, and sad. Those who've committed the act often need assistance in forgiveness and moving on to the other side where they'll be accepted.

———

I met Orson when Dale and Christine attended a paranormal investigation. Orson followed us around, curious, but afraid to speak up. I could tell he didn't belong to the location the way he was dressed, and then there was the fact he looked like a mini Dale.

"Is he suffering, Kristy?" Dale asked when I finally cornered them at the end of the night.

"He's suffering because you are," I honestly answered. "He doesn't deserve to relive the misery of life, nor do you. We have the choice to wallow in the emotional turmoil, but that doesn't help anyone."

"Is he regretful?" Christine asked. "I know I have all kinds of regrets," she said sitting down on a chair, putting her elbows in her lap. It'd only been six months since his suicide and emotions were raw.

"I want to come home," Orson said, "but I know that's not possible. I just don't want to hurt anymore. I re-live that day over and over, seeing different scenarios that I could've done, but instead I thought that I and them would be better without me."

"Oh, my God, son. I do the same thing," Dale cried. "Every moment of the day, I wish I could turn back the clock. Not yell at him. Take out my anger on someone else, because in the end it had nothing to do with a D on a test. I wish ... well, I wish for a lot that will never come true."

Christine took Dale's hand in hers. I was glad they hadn't played the blame game and they were helping one another. I have seen that more times than not couples will separate or divorce after a tragedy. I could see the cords that were still connecting the two together, and they were wound tight, meaning the marriage would last.

"So what does he see?"

Orson exclaimed that it was like he was living here on earth, only nobody could see him, feel him, or hear him. Once in a while he could see his grandpa who had passed, but the walk felt long and instead he just didn't take the effort.

"That's just like him. That's the argument we had here."

"It's not that he's lazy," I assured them, "It's that he doesn't feel worthy."

"So he's homeless?" Christine asked.

I nodded. "In a way. He can go find his eternal home if he chooses, but he has to know he's worth that." I shifted to Orson. "How can we help?"

"Can I still visit?" Orson asked, looking very much like his ten-year-old human years.

"You can. In fact you can visit easier once you cross," I shared. "Do you see a light?"

Orson nodded that he did. "Should I start walking there?"

I looked over at his parents to make sure they were on board. "I want him to have peace," Dale said. "I didn't give him that peace at the end, but I want to try and do what I can now."

Orson walked down a pathway until he said he saw his cat that passed when he was five years old, and his grandpa who was standing there in wait.

"Peace out, my boy."

Orson turned around and smiled. "Tell dad I said peace out back." Then he stepped through the threshold to the other side.

A year later I saw Dale and Christine at a local supermarket and we exchanged polite talk.

"Thanks for helping Orson find his heaven. He's visited a few times, we have no doubt."

I smiled and as I left I heard, "Peace out," only to turn around and Dale and Christine were already down another aisle. Orson found his peace.

Chapter Thirteen
Suicide and the Other Side

It seems several times a year we see announcements of actors and musicians, beloved by their fans, committing suicide—shaking many as such a personal and tragic ending. In the world of social media, it doesn't take long for a myriad of wildfire-like opinions, insensitive comments, and advice to pop up.

Mental illness and depression are real and true. Suicide doesn't kill, depression does. Depression and suicide seem to sadly be a synonymous theme with comedians. They try to make light of their inner demons by making fun of them. In reality, they are just smiling through the pain and not battling or healing at all. A smile or a laugh can only temporarily hide depression, and depression doesn't discriminate—the poor, rich, male, female, gay, straight, blue, and purple are all effected.

My mother had manic depression and no matter how many times we begged her to be happy, or how many times we tried to show her how much she had around her to be grateful for, she couldn't see down the dimly lit road of depression. When I was thir-teen years old, she lost her sight. Something I thought was sadly ironic. It is exhausting being a family member of someone with the disease (and yes, it is a disease), but just as exhausting for the one suffering. You can't simply tell a depressed person to be happy. You can't convince a depressed person that there is meaning in their life.

Each time a celebrity takes their life I see people asking why that person never asked for help, vocalizing judgment for hurting his/her family by doing the selfish act of suicide. Many times those who are suicidal do ask for help, but not always in the way we think. Sometimes, though, because of the wide range of judge-ment, people are afraid to ask, especially if you are in the spotlight.

———

Packing boxes isn't ever fun, but we were thrilled to be moving so we tried to make it as fun as we could. I've never been one to have someone else do it, the strong willed Scorpio that I am. So I packed, lifted heavy boxes, moved heavy boxes, and tried to do my part. The prize was a beautiful country home and tennis elbow.

Tennis elbow, or lateral epicondylitis, is a painful condition that occurs when the tendons in your elbow are overloaded, usually be-cause of repetitive motions of the wrist and arm. The pain can spread to your forearm, your wrist and even your fingers. Rest and over-the-counter pain relievers is often the treatment, but rest isn't something I do well. I did seek medical treatment and I wore a brace, and I got massages (which helped), took Ibuprofen like M&Ms, used essential oils, and so on. My sleep was disturbed (as I have a tendency to sleep on my stomach with my arm underneath me) and as time progressed the pain worsened, my fingers numbed.

Picking up objects resulted in them immediately dropping, and even typing was excruciating. I couldn't take it anymore so my husband Chuck took me to the nearest Urgent Care. They told me that it was severe and that I had so much inflammation that they gave me a pain shot, a steroid shot, and an oral steroid called Dexamethasone that I was to start the following day and take for six days, with the possibility of a refill after that. The injections took my pain away and I felt human again, until the following day when it wore off, so I began the oral steroids as prescribed.

The day after taking my first dose I began to feel angry. I was mad, I was sad, and I was confused, and simply chalked it up to sleep deprivation and stress. The third day of taking the medication resulted in me starting to see things that weren't there. Okay, so I see people who've crossed, but this felt weird and scary. It was different. My speech was slurred and I thought maybe I was having a stroke. Again, I let it go. The fourth day I was raging angry and my husband Chuck and I got into a huge fight over something ridiculous. To be honest I don't have a clue what it was even about now; it was that stupid. As he stormed out of the house, though, my thoughts turned dark.

Just kill yourself.

I didn't want to kill myself. I didn't want to leave my family and friends, but I wasn't thinking straight. I wasn't me. I felt like the only way to end the pain was to end my life. The devil on one shoulder was telling me to end my life and that nothing was going to get better or seem any better. The angel on the other shoulder was telling me this was a fleeting thought because something else was the matter and to just take a hot shower, drink some hot tea, and sleep off the mood.

I wanted to talk to someone, but I didn't want to go to a psych ward. I didn't want to be thought of as crazy. I had no idea who to call and at that moment I felt like nobody would care anyhow, even though I have a great tribe of family and friends who I know do care. But all I heard in my head was to end my life and get it over with. I thankfully listened to the angel on my shoulder, and after some hot tea and a gut wrenching sob I fell asleep on the couch.

The next morning I told Chuck that I needed to see the doctor, and so after work (yes, I was working during these crazy episodes) I went to my primary and explained to the nurse and the doctor as to what was happening, only to get the explanation that it was a side effect of the steroid and was called steroid psychosis. Not only was I having steroid rage, my hips, back and knees hurt like something I've never had before, and my eyesight was blurry. Even after discussing the suicidal feelings, I was nonchalantly told to drink a lot of water and wait for it to work its way out of my system, which could be two more weeks. Thankfully it was much less than that and I used that time of wait to re-ground myself with gardening, reading, and journaling.

Everyone's soul makeup is different and for a bit I was upset that I had to go through what I went through only to be told it was to help me understand those who've felt suicidal and those who have committed suicide. I got a glimpse of the numbness and deep emotional ache that their spirits have communicated to me in previous sessions.

Many say those who commit suicide are selfish, but as I went through the medicated haze I didn't have time to really feel. I didn't have the motivation to write a letter or to reach out to a toll free suicide hotline. I couldn't explain my emotional pain to my best friend, my husband. It was like my soul had abandoned me and the only way to find peace was to chase after it. I didn't think of the pain the loss would've caused my family, only that I had to go and find me again even if death was the only way. My moment was thankfully temporary and I'm back to me, albeit my elbow still hurts, but I'll take that over the psychotic episodes.

Being a medium, I've connected many people to loved ones they lost to suicide. I grew up in the Lutheran church, being told that anybody who commits suicide goes to hell and is punished. That isn't necessarily what I see on the other side, however. No matter how we pass, we must all go on a soul journey, or counseling of sorts that I call Angel Boot Camp, in order to heal. It isn't all fun and games and angel wings. My experiences with those on the other side who've committed suicide have been as different as each individual's life. Some have regrets, and some don't. Some aren't in the best place on the other side, although I wouldn't exactly define it as hell, and others transition just fine and are at peace with their decision. There is, however, no escape from our problems on this side or the next. I believe that lessons can be learned in all situations. Compassion has become a lost art in our society, which scares me. We must stop judging everyone, and we must stop judging those who may be broken inside! You never know what they are facing behind that smile!

I don't believe suicide is an answer, but at that moment in time for many, living is a so-called selfish act for those caught up in the depression. They feel that their tormented soul isn't just hurting themselves, but also their loves ones. And there is often truth in that because it does. When you can see potential within someone and they can't see that for themselves, it stings. Margaret Thatcher said,

"You may have to fight a battle more than once to win it." Life is a constant battle; add depression to it, the weight is even heavier.

I know there's more than one of you who have thought of leaving before your time. Some of you who may have even attempted to end your life at one time. There are some of you who now look at old pictures, dusty memories of someone you loved who couldn't face the pain anymore. No real explanation or a goodbye; they simply left the living wondering if there was something more that could've been done. There are some of you who face the challenges of getting up, pasting a smile on your face and doing a routine some call life, going to sleep and doing it all over again. You make it look easy, but really it's the hardest thing in the world and you don't want anyone to know the monsters you face along the way. To those of you who are still fighting the fight, I believe in you. To those of you who won the fight, I'm glad you are still here. To those of you mourning over a loss from suicide, I love you, and I know your loved one on the other side does too. If you are facing depression and contemplating suicide, there is help, and so often the help is more readily available than in the afterlife.

My wish for everyone is that within tragedy, suffering and sadness, you can find the rainbows. They are there, but you have to stop staring at the storm clouds. Yes, life's difficult. If it wasn't, the rainbows wouldn't be so special. If you can't find the rainbows, ask for help. If you are in crisis, call the National Suicide Prevention Lifeline at 1-800-273-TALK (8255).

If you are having your own moment, please know that you are wanted *here*. Even if you feel as if your soul has left. It hasn't, and there are people who want to help reconnect you to you again. It's not time for your story to end. It's okay to feel like a mess, and to admit that you are lost. If someone won't listen, find someone who will.

To all those who've lost their will to fight the battle, may you find your peace and fly with the angels.

Soul Loss and Fragments

Soul loss or fragmentation can occur as we reincarnate or during our current incarnation. It often happens when there are repetitive patterns of abuse, often unresolved. The trauma and the fears can be a heavy weight to hold and it begins to break pieces of the soul. While some seek help, learning how to step away from being the victim and finding their inner brave, many turn to drugs, others to alcohol, depression, and others to further damaging relationships. Some commit suicide, seeing the burden too heavy to bear.

Those with old souls carry the heaviest weight of lifetimes before, with possible lifetimes ahead. Abuse or trauma can attach to the soul, creating holes in the auric field which allows the darkness to saturate the light within, clouding the ability to see anything other than sadness and despair.

Shamans conduct what is called Soul Retrievals, often with their power animal. They call on the pieces of the lost soul and return them back to their place. Like an ethereal puzzle, the shaman practitioner helps to seek out the best parts of the soul most vital for healing. Inviting them back and even healing them with light, crystals, and prayers, it's important for the client to be willing for the reconnection and accepting of the gift.

I often see this fragmented soul in those who feel suicidal or who have committed to their life ending.

Signs of Soul Fragments

- Depression
- Emotionally numb
- Sleep disturbances
- Feeling worthless
- Low energy
- Low immune system
- Anxiety
- Fears
- Feeling surrounded by "bad" luck
- Feeling a loss of identity
- Not wanting to take action, feeling stuck
- Panic

Overall, it's a sign of feeling like you've lost yourself. It might happen over time, it might feel like you were never you from the beginning of time.

You don't need a shaman, however, but you do need to be willing to want to make a shift in your life. There's no magic potion or meditation that will solve your life problems. It's continued action.

Soul Retrieval Meditation

Take some time to relax your body and relax your mind. The more you are unaware of your body during this time, the easier it is for you to concentrate with your mind on just relaxing.

Take a deep breath, hold it for a moment, and slowly let it out. Allow all your tension to leave your body; with each breath out you release, and with each breathe in you take in joy, hope, love, and peace.

Imagine with every breath a very large, white ball of light moving toward you, closer and closer, getting larger and larger, and surrounding every part of you like walking into a cloud. It relaxes you from the tips of your toes to the top of your head, encouraging you to release, relax, and let go of what isn't serving you in this lifetime or other lifetimes.

"I accept this white light as my armor."

Now surrounded by white light, a shield that is your constant protector, call on your power animal. If you don't know who that is, call on your favorite animal. It can be anything from mythological like a unicorn or a passed pet. Then call on Archangel Michael, the warrior angel who wants to help assist you.

"I ask my guides, angels, Divine, and anyone of the higher light to help retrieve my soul pieces. I ask they be retrieved gently, timely, and with care for all concerned. So let it be. My gratitude for what is and what will be."

It may take a few times for you to do this until you begin to feel it. You can repeat this as often as you want. Sometimes recording yourself and playing it back at nighttime can be useful. Take that white light with you always, throughout your days and nights accepting the protection that you deserve.

Note that this isn't a replacement for medical care or diagnosis, or for psychiatric help.

Life tragedies often break off the fine china of the soul. You deserve to stop feeling as if this is your living hell and to find your heaven on earth so that you don't have to carry the baggage of this lifetime into your afterlife. I'd rather go on my flight without a carry-on, but rather dance to the other side, and spend more time reuniting and enjoying heaven.

Chapter Fourteen
A Ghost of a Reading

Most people visualize a ghost in the context of a translucent figure, or a shadow seen from the corner of the eye. You might hear a dis-embodied voice saying your name in a long and drawn out voice. "Krrrrriiiissssstttttyyyyyyy …" The room grows cold and you might see your breathe in the chill. Or it might not be that way at all, and simply be hype from paranormal shows and spooky movies.

It was a frosty autumn morning and the furnace in my office building hadn't yet been turned on for the season, so I plugged in my space heater and lit some candles hoping to warm up before my first appointment. I had just set my lighter down when my client rapped on the door.

"I think I'm a half hour early or so," the cheerful voice said, "I can just sit in your waiting room until you're ready," he suggested.

I was an early bird and was almost always early getting to the office, so there was no need for Nelson to wait. I introduced myself with a gentle handshake and gestured for him to have a seat. Grabbing a bottled water from my mini-refrigerator, I held up another for Nelson, but he shook his head and waved it off.

"Trying to cut back," he smiled. "Anything stronger?" he joked.

"Can't say there is," I replied with a teasing sigh. Taking a seat myself, I opened my water and set it next to me on the blue end table.

Nelson allowed himself to curiously look around the office. "Not quite what I expected," he simply said.

My office was whimsical with neutral furniture but decorated with soft blankets and colorful throw rugs. I hoped that it was comforting and had a happy vibe for my clients. Most times it was the men who felt the need to comment, ironically.

"Did your wife send you?" I asked, remembering a note in my online file mentioning something about the appointment for her husband.

"No," Nelson quickly added, sorrowful.

"Oh, okay, I must be mistaken," I stumbled. I was sure I saw that note. "Have you ever had a session done, Nelson?"

I picked up an onyx worry stone and stroked it slowly between my thumb and index finger as Nelson watched every movement.

"Nope, I never have. It was my daughter, Sharon, who thought I would benefit from seeing if you could connect to my wife, Esther."

I squinted at him, as if trying to read the fine print on instructions only to realize they were in a foreign language. I have a set of rules for when I tune into the spirit world so as to communicate it properly back to my clients. On my left I see those who've crossed over to the other side. To the right it is the energy of the people in the physical. Sometimes I have what is called the gray area, and I tend to see that at my ten o'clock position. These are energies who haven't crossed over, or sometimes just those who feel they might not be invited to the party of a session. I've had everyone from exes to old bosses show up. Today I had an energy that my guides told me was Nelson's daughter. But Nelson told me his daughter set up the appointment. To my right, my physical, I felt Nelson's wife, Esther. Sometimes spirit liked to play tricks on me, but it was normally those who were rule breakers or mavericks in spirit, and I don't get that feeling out of Nelson or his family. I was confused, but didn't want to admit it. Instead, I begged my guides to help me out.

"And you have just one daughter, right?" I asked Nelson.

"I do. Esther and I doted on her something else. We gave her anything she wanted. It wasn't until later that we realized that wasn't the way to parent."

"Your mom is here in spirit, Nelson. She said she passed when you were sixteen years old from a …" I tried to listen closely to the spirit, and thankful that someone was following along to my instructions. Nelson's mom was standing to my left and seemed to be chatty, but also agitated. "She says she passed from a heart attack and afterward your dad's health declined."

Nelson nodded. "That was so long ago," he said wiping his eyes. "I still miss them every day."

I'm privy to the stories of the living and the stories of the dead. Some are gut wrenching, but I try to keep my own emotions intact or else I'd look like Alice Cooper with mascara running down my face most days, waterproof or not. There was something about Nelson where I couldn't help but get misty at his gentle and raw soul. You could tell that even through all of his losses, he hadn't allowed himself to harden, and he communicated his feelings. It was rare to see in any generation. Nelson had a specialness to him, but through his eighty-something years, I don't think he recognized it in himself. There wasn't an ego. What you saw from Nelson was Nelson.

"Your mom loved your pick in Esther," I smiled. "They have similar energy."

"They certainly did, Kristy. I'm sure it was what drew me to Esther in the first place." He smiled back. "Esther had a quick laugh, quite melodic. She came from nothing. Her parents died in a car crash when she was a toddler and she was given to an aunt. She probably had her all of ten minutes before dropping her off at the local orphanage. She couldn't be bothered. Es grew up in that orphanage."

"I can't imagine," I said shaking my head.

"Do you know that not once did she talk badly about her aunt? And if you asked her about her childhood she would say she was provided for, without mention of the orphanage or her experiences. I know she didn't tell me everything, but I never pressed her. Instead we created our life with going forward and not back. We saw the destruction of our friends who were living in the past and mourning what couldn't come back; all the same losing the present and having just more to mourn for."

"And your mom came from nothing too, she says. I can see the similarities between the two for sure."

"Both mom and Es had heart issues, and that's what I lost them both from. I think they both cared so much. And you know what, Kristy? People who care so much are often run over by those who don't care much at all. It's like a gravel road after it rains. The bedrock is washed away or loosens with the constant travel, and creates deep pockets of pot holes. Mom and Es had a lot of potholes, but kept filling them in, pretending that everything was okay. It wasn't. It wasn't," Nelson repeated, his chin down into his chest.

"Esther loves you, though, Nelson. You didn't create the potholes. Well, maybe one or two, but that's called marriage."

Nelson lifted his chin and laughed. "Marriage isn't easy, and add in a kid or two or three like we have, and its sleepless nights from the get go."

I looked up again to see if the energy of the people had been corrected, but they were still placed the way I saw them in the beginning. The energy of Esther was still in the living here area and their daughter on the other side. I was grateful for Nelson's mom for coming through and helping so I decided to ask her about his daughter Sharon, who was still in the gray area. Instead of a response, his mom hung her head in sorrow and shook her head as if she couldn't answer. I was going to take a chance with a question I felt was on mark, but was worried Nelson would be upset.

"Nelson, did Sharon have a substance abuse problem? Had she attempted suicide before?"

Being an empath, I feel everything. Whether it is prescription or illegal drugs, I can feel it and Sharon's energy felt submerged in an overload of toxins. I could also feel the ache on my arm from the needles.

Nelson hung his head, duplicating his mom's sorrow.

"You have nothing to be ashamed of," I counseled. "You were always a fabulous dad to her. Always."

I looked at Sharon, who I saw in spirit, and she nodded at me in agreement. I knew then she had passed, and by her own hand, but I was confused why Nelson wasn't being truthful with me. He seemed like a genuine and honest person.

Some clients will play tricks on me by changing their names, taking their wedding rings off, or putting fake wedding rings on. I try to be as authentic with my work as I can be, honest and a straight shooter. I don't ever want to mislead or say something to give them immediate happiness, knowing it isn't what I'm truly seeing, and I expect the same from my client. I don't want to play pretend, and it's exhausting for a client to try and trick me. It honestly blocks the flow of energy and pollutes the session. I didn't feel that Nelson was intentionally doing this, but something was off. I just couldn't figure out what it was.

"Since Sharon's birth she was different. She felt more than others, always worried, always concerned about everyone else. She rarely smiled, and always seemed to have a dark cloud that shrouded her. Then she came home from college the end of junior year to tell us that she found her soulmate. We were happy for her. It was her first real and true love. We were cautious, but she just glowed and she seemed so happy. We were disappointed when she dropped out of school to marry the fella, but we liked him and he had gotten a great job. He assured and reassured us that he'd take care of her and he'd get her back into school, but then came Mari, their first baby girl. Something changed in Sharon, and the dark cloud began drowning her again," Nelson recalled.

"And then came a baby boy?" I asked.

Nelson nodded. "And then Mason came and Sharon was fine again. Or so we thought."

"And you didn't know about her addiction? I think you did know, though, Nelson."

Nelson's face paled. "It went in waves, and I suppose I never wanted to see it. I think she's good now, though," he quickly added.

"Is she?" I wondered to myself. I still saw her on the other side and if she hadn't passed, she was about to pass. It wasn't a message I felt I could help get through to Nelson, though, or maybe was supposed to. It was obvious he was in denial about Sharon's issues.

So I moved on to the next person in line on the other side that was waiting to talk to Nelson. Again, this one was in the space that denoted my other side, and Nelson validated that the next few people had in fact passed away.

The hour went by quickly, and as my alarm rang noting the time, Nelson hopped up to leave.

"Kristy, I really enjoyed this," Nelson smiled. "I didn't know what to expect, but this was nice. I'd like to come back sometime."

"I don't think I'll see you again," I blurted out loud.

I had no idea where it came from, but I was grateful Nelson didn't seem to be offended.

"Well, I hope you're wrong. I hope we meet up again." He gently touched my shoulder and then asked for a hug, of which I willingly gave him.

"You take care of yourself. And that beautiful daughter of yours too," I added. "Oh, and I know your wife loves you very much. You two will always be soulmates. There's no time or space when it comes to love."

Nelson hugged me tighter and wiped the tears from his ocean blue eyes and quietly nodded in understanding.

I opened my office where my next two clients were waiting for their session. Nelson was a tall and lean man, but there was something about him that seemed to take up so much space. He bumped into one of my client's legs and profusely apologized, only for her to laugh it off. It was just a harmless bump.

The three of us watched Nelson leave the hallway toward the front door before introducing myself to my newest clients and showing them into my office, praying that this session wasn't going to be so confusing.

The two ladies commented on how Nelson seemed like a gentle soul, and I nodded in agreement, careful to not break confidentiality. It was something I was particularly careful about. I don't much care if you were a celebrity on screen or a celebrity in the classroom; I don't read and tell.

Thankfully the rest of my day went without issue, and all the remainder of the spirits followed my instructions.

———

For years I used to carry the problems, grief, and sadness with me from my clients. The burden would eventually become so heavy that I would have an emotional breakdown, let it go, and start all over again. I finally couldn't do it anymore so I began the practice of washing the energy of my day off before coming home. Envision the *Men In Black* zap, although it really isn't that cool. What I do is wash my hands, take a deep breath, and imagine standing in bare feet with deep roots coming from my feet into the earth. Then I draw the energy up through the spiritual roots in my foot, and on my first exhale I envision the crystals of everyone's issues being healed and being carried off by the angels to assist. With my first inhale I ask for white light to wrap around me, then I mentally ask that any scattered bits of myself be brought back to me and that any dusty dark, or negative pieces be either cleaned or let go of. I turn the water off to the sink, take another deep cleaning breath and leave it all there. Often I'm asked days, weeks, or sometimes years later if I remember the session with their loved one, but because of my now practice I will only have bits and pieces, not a total recall.

There was, however, something about Nelson's session that no matter how much I tried to energy wipe, I just couldn't and it started to make sense as to why when I received a phone call the following week. It was a call from Nelson's wife, Esther.

"Kristy," the lady started with a pause, "This is Esther Parry. My husband Nelson had an appointment with you last week, dear, and I'm so very sorry that I didn't call you beforehand with the funeral arrangements and all," she rambled. "I know how much you dislike no-shows. I follow you on Facebook," Esther added. "Anyhow, Nelson had a massive heart attack and his funeral was the morning of his appointment. I should've called to re-schedule the appointment for me instead, but..."

I was listening, but I didn't comprehend what she was saying and instead of replying to her I hung up the phone and stared at it like it was about to bite me. I quickly looked up the number of one of the clients that came after Nelson and dialed the phone.

"Beth, this is Kristy," I said into the phone as soon as my client answered. "This is going to sound strange, but..." I thought for a moment how I wanted to word it, but no matter how, it was going to be weird. So I simply blurted it out. "You saw the older gentleman that came out of my office last week, right?"

"Yes, both Trudy and I did. In fact we had lunch after the session to just chat about what you said and we both mentioned how there was something...I don't know, special, about him. Neither of us could put our fingers on it."

"Okay, thanks so much, Beth," I said and without explanation promptly hung up the phone and hit re-dial on Esther's number.

As much as I wanted to fib and tell Esther my phone cut out, I knew that wasn't right or fair. I didn't, however, know what to say. Esther answered on the first ring.

"Esther, I apologize for that," I said, meaning it. "I'm so sorry to hear about Nelson, but …," I took a deep breathe before continuing. "I saw Nelson on the day of his appointment. He came to his appointment early, even. He was wearing a light blue shirt, with khaki slacks and he kept apologizing for coming early," I rambled.

"That's impossible, Kristy. Nelson's funeral was that same day at eleven. I've known you for a while, and I don't know you to be a joker, but if that's what you're doing it's not funny," she reprimanded.

I had been pacing as I spoke to her, but I sat down at my desk to try and gather my own thoughts. I was physically shaken.

"I'm not joking," I promised and shared with her the entire interaction, down to how his hair was combed, to his denial of their daughter's drug issue, and confessed that I hung up on her and called Beth and Tricia to validate that they too saw him. Esther was quiet for the most part, until it came to Sharon, and I could hear her try to silence her crying.

"Esther, did Sharon pass recently? He was adamant that you had passed and that he and Sharon were alive."

"Kristy, do you have a few minutes to chat in person?" Esther asked, without answering.

I had a library event that evening, so we set a time the following morning to meet at my office. Just like Nelson, Esther was early.

Visibly shaken, when I volunteered a seat for her, she asked me if that was where Nelson had sat. I told her it was and she began to sob. Although it wasn't a reading session, I called on Nelson's spirit to come through, but instead it was Sharon who stood there. Standing again in my gray area, her energy felt stiff and icy.

"Nelson found Sharon's body," Esther blurted out. "For so long we tried to get her help, every which way, with every means we could afford. There were many sacrifices and ultimately I lost my husband as the final sacrifice."

I looked over at Sharon's spirit, still aloof and void.

"Nelson died from a broken heart, didn't he?"

"The morning after Sharon's funeral I woke up and Nelson was still sleeping. It was unusual for either of us to sleep in, but we'd been so emotionally exhausted that I just left him there and began to fix our coffee and some breakfast; a poached egg, rye toast, and turkey bacon. We were trying to watch what we ate," she explained staring off into the memory. "Then it was as if someone pushed me over to the bedroom to check on him again, and I found that he wasn't sleeping." Esther's voice cracked. "Nelson had died during the night. He looked so peaceful. The paramedics said he probably didn't suffer. He just slipped away."

As I listened on I couldn't help my own tears. As strong as Esther sounded, her energy was riddled with regrets, resentments, confusion, love, and horror.

"You really saw Nelson?" Esther whispered.

I nodded to her as I wiped my face. "I think I gave a reading to a ghost," I confessed.

"But how? He's not in heaven then? He's not at peace then?"

I could hear Esther silently screaming, suffocating with each breath she took as she held on to her pride, her sanity. As she asked the questions her mind reeled with the worst possibilities.

Her questions, though, were the same questions I had. I felt that Sharon was the key to most everything and she simply stood there, without reaction.

Finally, Sharon spoke. "Nobody understood me. The depression. The addiction. It's not just something you can wish away, it's an actual feeling. It's a feeling that you try to find the remedy for the itch, but all that does is invoke dark clouds that drown you. There's no air. There's no sight. You push, and you push, pretending to be normal, whatever that is, feeing the feeling that you aren't sure is real or not.

"Ever since I was six years old I would wake up hoping I was dead. I didn't want a puppy. I didn't care about school trips or birthday parties. I just thought I'd be better off dead. As I got older I let things distract me into pushing that feeling away, the itch I so badly wanted to scratch. I wanted to give in to the power of it most days, but I didn't want to hurt anyone. Each day I faced the challenges and each day the suicidal thoughts got louder. The demons spoke louder than the angels and not even the medication could expel the slivers that went deeper and deeper into my soul until I finally had to bleed it out of me."

"At the expense of your father," Esther screamed after I shared Sharon's message. Clenching her fists in her lap, she fell into uncontrollable sobs. "At the expense of me too." All I could do was embrace Esther and let the torrent of her tears soak through my shirt. Esther clutched the delicate gold cross that hung from her neck. "I'm sorry," she choked.

There was no need to apologize, though, and honestly I just wanted to see if I could help Sharon, and Nelson, cross over, and hopefully find their peace. I moved back to my chair after Esther composed herself.

Esther and Nelson had three children, Sharon was their only daughter, and it was obvious in my session with Nelson that Sharon was special to him. Not necessarily a favorite, but they had a special bond. I wondered if Esther was perhaps a tad bit jealous of Nelson and Sharon's relationship. It would seem that Sharon's issues derailed money, time, and energy away from her and their sons, and now it became permanent with Nelson gone.

"Dad was the only one who helped me out," Sharon shared, as if reading my mind. "Mom, not so much. She hated every part of me."

I didn't think that was true, but I shared the message nonetheless.

"I loved her more than my own self," Esther opposed. "I would've traded places if it could've taken away any of her pain and depression.

"Oh, please," Sharon whispered under her breathe. "She's a narcissist and always has been."

I had a challenging relationship with my own mother. I thought I was always right. She thought she was always right, and we rarely met in the middle. When we are children, we require our parents to give us support, encouragement, nurturing, and love, but that doesn't always happen and those that are denied that learn how to cope in any way they can. My support system was books and journaling. Sharon's support system was a drug dealer and needles.

I couldn't determine if Esther was a narcissist. I wasn't a licensed therapist, and, to be honest, name calling or labels wouldn't help at all anyhow. I also decided against sharing that message. It was neither helpful nor healing for anyone.

"Sharon, have you seen your dad?" I asked her out loud.

Esther leaned forward in her seat in wait.

"For a moment, and then he was gone," she said, her voice turning hard.

"Is he lost, Kristy? What's happening?" Esther asked.

Maybe Nelson crossed over and Sharon was stuck in between. Maybe there were different layers of the in-between, like floors of a high rise. I was determined to figure it out. I continued to call on Nelson, or anyone else for Esther, but nobody came, only Sharon stood there, unhappy and angry. Just as I was about to tell Esther we'd have to re-convene her husband came through in spirit and, although I could see him, Esther could feel him.

"He's here, isn't he?" she asked, her eyes wide. "Is he touching my arm? I can feel him touching my arm," she cried.

He was touching her arm. His eyes bright with tears. His energy radiated love, but also a tinge of regret.

"Are you crossed, Nelson?" I asked.

He nodded that he was.

"Can you see Sharon?" Esther asked.

"I can't," he muttered wistfully.

"I think that you both need to forgive yourself. I think that you both need to forgive each other. And I think you both need to forgive Sharon. There are walls up around each one of you, Sharon included, but I think her soul is fragmented like Humpty Dumpy. All the pieces are there, and it's not up to you to put her back together again. It's up to her," I emphasized, darting my response her way.

"How do we do that?" Esther asked.

Just as I was about to shrug my shoulders in defeat, a crowd of spirits came through and stood in back of Nelson, creating a heavenly posse filled with information to help.

"Nelson and Esther, can you think of an incident that made you angry regarding Sharon that you feel you re-live over and over?" They both nodded. "Can you look back on the incident and forgive yourself and anyone else connected with that. You can even say it out loud. 'I forgive you.'"

Although Esther and Nelson were in different energy planes, they spoke the words in unison. "I forgive you."

"Sharon, they would like you to do the same."

Sharon looked over at me like the enemy.

"Sharon, can I ask you what you see where you are?"

"I have work to do still," she sighed without any detail.

It wasn't the answer I was hoping for, but at least she was still here and still speaking to me.

"Maybe this is all part of your work, Sharon," I tried reasoning. "So can you recall the first time in your physical life that you were disappointed? This could be the key that is holding on to your recovery."

Sharon stared at me and grimaced.

"This is important," I pled.

"I just wanted love, but instead I was humiliated on a daily basis from the moment Seth was born."

"How old do you remember it happening for the first time?"

"I was six. I was only six and on a daily basis I was being told that I was dumb. I was told to stop crying. I just wanted love." Sharon shrilled. "She was supposed to be my refuge, but instead I searched for a hole to hide, to be as invisible as I could be. That wasn't even good enough. The criticism was daily."

I looked at both Nelson and Esther and I could tell that Sharon was telling the truth, however it was perceived worse than what it was. It was those hurtful, critical words early on that were her first dose of toxicity. Words help to mold and shape who you become, for good and for bad. And when it's negative, it's like poison.

Esther spoke, "I was overwhelmed. I had three babies under six years old. Nelson was working overtime to pay for everything and I was so tired that I didn't know what I was saying. I had my own depression. I suppose now they call it post-partum," Esther looked down at her hands before looking up at me. "I'm not a bad person, Kristy. I'm so sorry, Sharon," she said, looking around her as if willing herself to see her. "I tried tough love, but there was love. There was," Esther erupted into sobs.

Tough love to someone as sensitive as Sharon can turn toxic. Met with good intentions, it doesn't make the person dishing it out cruel and uncaring. We really get no handbook defining how to deal with every relationship we are handed. Sometimes we simply compromise ourselves and our happiness by trying to be, or trying really hard not to be, the person someone else wants us to be. Sharon died never really knowing who she was, or feeling her mother's love. Nelson, her father, was the buffer between the two. He too felt everything, much like his daughter, but he too had an addiction; his just wasn't a chemical one—it was work, and it gave him the space away from the drama that Sharon had to absorb and that Esther had to try and control.

Esther sat there empty of her tears.

"Sharon, can you forgive?" I hesitantly asked.

Her demeanor had shifted after her outburst. The icy energy turned into a vulnerable little girl just needing love, and needing forgiveness as well. Sharon didn't speak, instead I could feel the walls of hurt that had been built were falling and that was forgiveness. That was her barrier that was blocking the light within, and her light to walk in to get to the other side.

"Now, I want you each of you to say that you deserved better and you deserve better."

They all stood in their own strength and looked at the value each of their relationships offered, knowing that they were deserving of better, and worthy of more. Whether it was healthy or not, emotionally holding on to it was like holding one's breathe. It blocked their flow and their true selves.

"Sharon, you're strong enough and valuable enough to get through this and you're not alone. You were never alone. I love and want the best for you, even if that best is in heaven and not with me," Esther apologized with compassion. "I wish I could hold her one more time," she told me.

Before I could answer my office lights flickered and I could see a bright light, like a flashlight shining down a long hallway. I looked at Esther to see if she saw it only to see her engulfed in a ray of sunshine that had peeked through the curtains of my office window.

"I think that's your hug."

———

Three months after Nelson's session and my meeting with Esther I received word from Nelson and Esther's son that Esther had a heart attack. Despite attempts to revive her, her will was to be with her husband.

"As much as we are sad to have lost our mom, dad, and sister weeks apart, my brother and I are so grateful for all the help you gave them. Even through the grief, after mom met with you we noticed a difference. A calming. I hope that they are all getting a do-over on the other side."

It wasn't long after the note when I received a visit from all three of them. They all stood together, in the same energy field, side by side.

"You asked me what I saw before I crossed," Sharon spoke. "I said I had work to do, and I did, but I was too stubborn to do it here on earth, and when I died at my own hand I was too afraid to go into the light. The only way I can describe where I was in an earthly way is that it was like a waiting room. Everyone wanted to help, but I was afraid, I didn't trust, and I was angry.

Forgiveness is a hard life lesson, and can be a hard lesson on the other side as well, but it frees us from the pain. When I speak of forgiveness in my office, most have no idea where to start. They feel as if it is giving the person that wronged them an out for spewing the hurt. What regret, anger, and lack of forgiveness does, however, is hurt you, not the person that you need to forgive. The past can bind you so that you can't walk into the future, or into the afterlife.

Chapter Fifteen

The Surrender

When a person is in a coma or vegetative state, the soul of that person can still be very much there. The astral body, also known as the soul, can hover in and out of the physical body because it hasn't disconnected from the physical body. When the soul is connected to the physical, a physical response is often witnessed from eye movement, head turning, fingers wiggling, and so on. When the cord between the physical and spiritual is severed, the physical body cannot survive any longer and rarely responds. Spirits who had Alzheimer's have shared a similar explanation with me. Instead of their body not cooperating, though, it is the mind that overthinks disconnecting from their body. It truly is body, mind, and soul.

Letting Go

"We can't say for sure whether he'll emerge from this state or not," the doctor soberly told Carrie. "It could be days. It could be months. It could be years."

She didn't understand, though. Weren't doctor's supposed to know? Modern technology and medicine and all? It was all a bit too surreal and the late-twenty-year-old newlywed just wanted to wake from the nightmare.

TJ left for work like every morning. They rushed around, Carrie always late, and TJ always on time. A hurried kiss and he was out the door. Carried had just sat down at her desk at the fancy architecture firm she'd worked at for almost five years when the receptionist buzzed her phone and asked she come to the lobby.

"Probably flowers," she gushed to herself, smiling as she strutted up to the front. TJ was spontaneous and romantic like that. For Valentine's Day one year he dressed as a Teddy Bear, came to her work, and serenaded her. Despite working in the stereotyped manly construction field, TJ knew how to woo a woman, and he did it from the get go. Their wedding was overflowing with family and friends as they spoke from the heart, with their own vows. It was TJ's words that made everyone laugh and cry. Carrie joked that half of the women there were probably ex-girlfriends. He was just that nice and never tried to hurt anyone, even if he was breaking up with them. He wanted everyone to be his friend.

Carrie wasn't met by a delivery of flowers, instead it was two policemen. TJ had been sitting at a stop light on his way to a job site, he was shot in the head by a botched carjacking.

"He tried reasoning with the man instead of giving up the car," they told her as they rushed to the hospital.

TJ had emergency brain surgery to remove the bullet, and lay in the cold hospital room fighting for his life. Carrie couldn't comprehend how life changed in mere seconds. For almost two months TJ held on, each test looking graver.

"But he kind of squeezed my hand," Carried would reason with the response of sad looks from the nurses and doctors. "That was to mean something, right?"

It was decided on the eighth week that they would remove all the tubes and wires to see what happened, like some science experiment.

"Can I do anything to bring him back, Kristy?" Carrie asked at an emergency session. "A spell? Is there a way to barter with God, like giving up having children to get him in return?"

There was nothing like that, though. I sensed TJ hovering between sides, which made my message even more emotional.

"I've been healing my soul and spirit in order to make my journey," TJ told me. "I feel her. I see her, but it's not from my physical body, but outside of it. And sometimes I can respond. I don't want to leave, but I have to leave. I'm no good for anyone the way that I am now," he shared. "Tell her grandma Zia is here and wants to help her and me. And tell her I see Buffy, my favorite dog growing up. She's here too helping me cross over. And it's beautiful. It's so beautiful," his eyes sparkled with tears. "I want her here too, but it's not her time."

"It wasn't his time either," Carrie cried. "We have so much yet to do. We have kids to have and vacations to take, and …," she stopped to catch her breath. "It's not his time," she whispered falling into a heap of sobs.

"We will always be connected, but she has to let me go."

"How can that possibly be done?" she clenched her fingers into a fist and squeezed.

That night Carrie held TJ's hand, his whole family surrounded him, and they prayed that the cord of his soul be disconnected from the cord to his body, releasing him to take the journey to the other side.

"We all saw a bright blue light hovering over his body as he took his last breathe, and then move into the corner of the room. It simply disappeared," Carrie told me in an email. "The room was filled with what I can describe as an orgasmic sigh of happiness."

Many have witnessed the passing of their loved one, pets included, and shared experiences such as seeing a bright light around the body or shining in the room, the face changing from wrinkled to youthful, and the eyes shining bright. Some have smelled their loved one's favorite scent right when they pass, others have felt a sense of relief and happiness despite the sadness of the loss.

Alzheimer's—Between Two Worlds

Allesandro sat on the bed next to his grandmother as she lay dying. She suffered from Alzheimer's for almost ten agonizing years, and although everyone was sad about losing her to the other side, there was something soothing about knowing she would be whole again very soon.

Hospice was present, offering morphine and making certain she was comfortable and cared for. "She probably has another couple days," the nurse told Allesandro. "You can go home and rest and come back."

But Allesandro wasn't so sure. He knew they were the experts, but an hour before, his grandmother sat straight up in bed, and looking through him said, "Dorothy, I'll be there soon. Just wait,"

It was the first intelligent thing she'd said in months, everything else had been mumbling.

Dorothy was her sister who'd died over twenty years before.

"Grandma, is anyone else there?" he asked, gently, not wanting to press or upset her.

She nodded her head and whispered, "Grandpa's here. He's so handsome in his blue suit."

A picture in the living room was of his grandpa smiling and wearing a blue suit, surrounded by his prized tomatoes. Why he was wearing a suite in a garden was something Allesandro never asked, and now wished he had, but he loved that she was getting visitations, so he picked up the phone.

"Mom, I think grandma is going soon. I think you need to get here."

Hospice said otherwise, but as the time ticked, she was talking to more and more deceased loved ones and offering hints to what heaven would be like.

"I can't wait to see the beach again," she giggled. "Dorothy, we are going to have so much fun as long as Al lets me go." She looked over the other way and smiled. "Al said I can go!"

Returning to the now, she patted her grandson on his hand. "Sonny, can you turn off the light. It's so bright," she quipped using Allesandro's nickname from childhood. He hadn't heard her use it in ages.

But there was no light on.

"It's getting brighter, Sonny." Her voice growing soft and light, she closed her eyes, took a big deep sigh, and left.

———

"I felt an electric shock go through my body," he shared with me. "I just know it was her soul being released."

Allesandro's family didn't make it for their final goodbye, but they'd said their slow goodbyes over the last decade as her mind slipped.

Ways to Surrender to the Other Side

We are fighters by nature, taught to survive no matter. This often happens when tackling life and death. But sometimes we have to learn how to surrender and put down the broken sword in lieu of keeping up the constant fight.

Ways to surrender:

- Don't take life too seriously.
- Spend more time with good thoughts, release the bad thoughts.
- Let go of what isn't working.
- Build bridges instead of walls.
- Be kind, including to yourself.
- Think about what has upset you.
- Accept that it's happened.
- Check your reaction—are you mad, angry, sad.
- Feel it.
- Acknowledge the lesson in it.
- Know that you survived it.
- Say the words out loud—"I forgive you." "I surrender to the now so I can make room for the next."
- Be consistent.
- Live in the moment.
- Don't worry so much about quantity, but instead about quality.

Together Again

Inez was diagnosed with breast cancer when she was just a teenager, and beat it. Thinking she was in the clear, according to her doctors and her yearly exams, she went on with her life. She got married, became pregnant, and had a beautiful baby. It was after the birth and Joslyn wasn't getting enough milk when it was discovered that her cancer had come back. After just three months she surrendered to her battle with the cancer.

Inez was the breadwinner since her husband was disabled in the military years back. To put it bluntly, they were broke, and Leo scraped together just enough to pay for the funeral, but unsure of how to make the mortgage and car note for the next few months. I received an email from Leo begging me for an appointment. I receive many requests for free sessions, and unfortunately I can't accommodate most of them. There was, though, something about Leo that prompted me to ask him to meet me in my office.

Leo sat across from me, bouncing his beautiful eight-month-old daughter on his knee. It was amazing to see how much the little girl resembled her mom who stood right next to them in spirit. Obviously still grieving for his wife as it was just a few weeks since her passing, his wife asked me to tell him how proud she was of him for staying true to who he was, and for constantly talking to her.

"He was always a chatter box," she laughed. "As Joslyn will be. He's in for some trouble!"

Leo confirmed that he spoke to his bride several times a day, asking her everything from how to get stains out of clothes to how to make her homemade macaroni and cheese.

"I should have paid more attention," he cried, "but I do hear her. In my head."

Joslyn began to fuss so he stood up and began to pace, patting her back lovingly. "That probably sounds nuts."

I smiled and shook my head at him, "And you say this to the person who talks to those on the other side?" I teased.

He laughed, but quickly grew somber. "I only hear her when I let all expectations go; when I surrender. When I am upset or anxious, well, I don't hear her."

I nodded with understanding. We lose the connection when we're stressed, but when we surrender and stop controlling—the line of connection becomes clear. It's like we move from the dead zone to free Wi-Fi.

Inez actually hadn't yet crossed over when I met with Leo. She was still caught in the middle, the in-between. Some believe "in-between" is technically a ghost-like state.

When we pass we go through a series of steps, the first is the soul, or life review. After the soul review you get to make the decisions as to what is next. Some choose to quickly reincarnate and others decide to take time to reflect. Some decide to do what is called a soul split, which is leaving a piece of the soul in heaven and incarnating another piece. Those who decide to stick around choose what their heaven is and who it includes, as long as it coincides with the other soul too. This step can take six to twelve months, which gives their loved ones time to unpack, get settled, and find their voice once more. After all, without a physical body, we don't have vocal chords to talk, right? We are also given an opportunity to help others. This may come in the means of being someone's Spirit Guide or a loved one's Guardian. It could also be an occupation in heaven, but whatever it is will be something you choose and you will love. You won't ever get that "Oh no, it's Monday!" feeling here.

Sometimes it takes two to three earthly weeks for a spirit to make it over the threshold so they can move through the steps. Inez's reason for not completely crossing wasn't fear of judgement, it was that she didn't want to leave her family and she felt as if she was being punished.

"I'm with them, but not with them. I feel so frustrated," she said. "Are you sure I can still visit once I cross completely?"

Inez paced along with her husband, memorizing every feature of her baby girl's face from her dark locks to her button nose.

"My wife is a … ghost?" Leo swallowed hard. "Can I help her?"

"You have to start believing that you'll be okay, and that your little one will be okay. Not just say it, but believe it."

Leo slouched back into the seat, Joslyn now asleep in his arms. "But I don't, Kristy. I don't know if I'll be okay."

"Then you are both in the middle," I warned. "Can I help you help yourself, which in turn helps her?"

Leo held his hand up in protest, realizing it wasn't going to help. I was going to share anyhow.

I had a couple ideas that might help him out financially, and thought if Inez knew he wasn't going to live out of a refrigerator box, and Joslyn wouldn't end up in foster care, she'd be able to move forward.

"I want to see you in three weeks. This time and date, okay?" I handed him a reminder card and took a second to stroke the baby's cheek, which felt like it was kissed by heaven. "You help you, you help her."

Leo didn't make his appointment, though. Two days later I saw the article in the newspaper.

Tragedy strikes a family twice in just a month. 35 year-old Leo Linghman and his infant daughter Joslyn died when a 75-year-old driver failed to stop for a red light on Broadway Street. Just a month back, Leo lost his wife to cancer. Funeral arrangements are still being made by family member.

Several months later I was sitting in my office when I caught sight of Leo and Inez. Inez held close her baby daughter. No words were spoken, they simply smiled and waved. This time I could tell they'd crossed over to heaven, together.

Have you lost your connection? Have you lost your faith?

Yogi Bhajan said, "You surrender to a lot of things which are not worthy of you. I wish you would surrender to your radiance … your integrity … your beautiful human grace."

It isn't just about being persistent, but being consistent, in everything you do, including talking to your loved ones on the other side, prayer, ethics, etc.

Sometimes surrendering is just another way of forgiving. Leo knew that Inez didn't want to pass and leave them, but there was an anger that had rooted. It wasn't toward her, it was toward life. His moving on, however, would be to the other side with his beautiful bride. Inez hadn't moved on because she was waiting for the reunion to move on together.

Chapter Sixteen

With Heaven's Help

It was my last speaking event of 2013. Although I was exhausted and working on fumes, I was grateful for the work. October is my busiest time of the year as many think of psychics during that month of Halloween. It was something I found odd and amusing, but I have adjusted to the ebb and flow of the field. This lecture was on hauntings of Michigan and I had probably given it a couple dozen times just that month and I was on autopilot. This one was a bit different. This speaking engagement was at the library next door to my old employer and I knew that past coworkers would be attending so I had to be as on as I could be. With standing room only, I was grateful for a large presence, and sure enough after the presentation several old friends and the curious came up to say their hellos. One couple stood back from the crowd, allowing everyone else to leave. The gentleman had been at my presentation at another library the night before, and although I recognized him as a Facebook friend, we had never personally met that I knew of. The night before he briefly introduced himself to me as Mick. I liked his energy. He had a curious nature, and compassionate eyes that seemed to be filled with hidden concern. This night he had what I assumed was his wife with him, and sure enough as Chuck and I began to pack up my books, Mick walked up and introduced me to Cindi, his wife. I could immediately tell why the two were partners with their yin and yang balance. Cindi was a pretty lady with short brown hair, hazel eyes, and although seemed sensitive she was appropriately guarded. She seemed self-assured and unapologetically confident having years of fending for herself. Her husband didn't hide his nervousness and sensitivity as well as she. He wore his heart on his sleeve, and it didn't take a psychic to see that.

As the four of us walked together out to the parking lot they asked if they could share a concern they wondered and hoped I could help with.

A few weeks before, Mick and his mom took a road trip to see a lecture from a medium who only sees spirits who are stuck in the in-between. During the lecture she called out the fact that in the in-between people seem to have unfinished business before they can cross, but they will cross eventually; they might just need some help. As Mick walked away the Medium stopped him in his tracks.

"Albert is with you."

"I don't have an Albert," he replied, turning around and facing the woman.

"Well, he's here and he says he's buried in Glenwood Cemetery."

Instead of asking any further questions, Mick left, confused and stunned as to who she was referring to.

Albert? He thought on his drive home. It wasn't Albert, it was Adelbert, his father-in-law. It sure sounded very close to Albert. He was in fact buried in Glenwood Cemetery. His drive back home was anguishing. How was he supposed to tell his wife that her father wasn't in heaven? He could kick himself for having a brief episode of amnesia and now, he felt, he missed his opportunity to hear more or figure out what to do. Then he remembered he had a local medium on his Facebook and decided to make sure I wasn't crazy.

"Is he really not crossed over, Kristy?" he asked me underneath the clear autumn sky.

Those who haven't crossed over look different to me. They aren't solid, they are wispy and translucent. Standing next to Cindi was in fact a male energy that looked just like that. No, he hadn't crossed over and I wanted to help him. I wanted to help Mick and Cindi. Whether her father would cross over or not was another story. There are many reasons why a spirit decides to not go into the light, and I had a feeling that there wasn't just one reason here, but several.

Chuck and I made plans to meet Mick and Cindi the following day at Glenwood Cemetery, about an hour away from our home. Cindi's brother would join us remotely—as he resided in another state, and I would hopefully cross their father over.

The afternoon was warm for a November. We sat beside his gravestone and with a sage stick, lighter, and Cindi's brother on FaceTime. The five of us began with prayer. I could feel Cindi's father hovering, unhappy and even frightened, an emotion I don't think he demonstrated often. He wasn't a happy person in life and I think he'd hoped that when he passed he might find some peace. He wished, perhaps, all of his life wrongs would be made right.

Cindi's upbringing was difficult, thus the guardedness that I saw around her when we first met. Adelbert was the head of the household, rarely showing his compassionate or loving side to his family. Mick found irony in his father-in-law being around him as he was the first to explain that Adelbert just didn't like him. Although I didn't see that he was sharing the adversarial relationship in spirit, I actually saw that his father-in-law was a tad jealous of Mick's happy-go-lucky and carefree energy, something he could never find in this lifetime. Adelbert could be controlling, and Mick wouldn't be controlled. Mick's family was much like Mick himself, and in a way I could see that Adelbert envied that mellow spirit that he, himself, never found.

Adelbert was a charismatic man and was loved by those who didn't truly know him. To those who *did* know him, he had a boisterous, strong willed, and always right personality. His stoic European upbringing and heavy drinking brought out the fear in his family to be cautious and walk on egg shells. There are happy alcoholics, and mean alcoholics, and Adelbert erred on the side of the latter. Although not a monster, he was his own worst enemy and made those closest to him pay for it in spades. Adelbert made it known that he was the head of the family and because he was the provider he wanted to be treated with admiration. It wasn't earned, but demanded.

After Cindi's mom and Adelbert's wife passed he married Helga. Not the kind hearted, loving wife and mother he was graced with before, but someone very angry and similarly demanding.

For hours Helga held Adelbert's hand begging and pleading for him not to leave. Commanding him, even, that death shouldn't be able to conquer through his armor of strong will, knowing all too well that the fight was ending.

"Don't go," she screamed on his last earthly day. Angry that he wasn't listening to her, knowing that death was near, she left and went home to agonize over what she'd do afterward.

It was Cindi, with her brother by her side, who stayed by their father's side during his last moments, reconciling the difficult relationship, but understanding why it was that way. Cindi wanted the best for her father and prayed for a happy afterlife, one that he deserved to find and never found on earth. She whispered, "Dad, go to Mom. Dad, you have to go find Mom."

A spiritual battle ensued. The earthly cords that Helga had wrapped around Adelbert throughout their years together, along with Adelbert's own fear of judgement and justice, was the reason he stayed bound to the in-between even after his body finally gave into the abyss.

I could feel Cindi's father hovering, unhappy. He wasn't a happy person in life either and I think he believed once his physical didn't exist that it would magically go away. That all the life wrongs, and his regrets, would simply evaporate into ashes like his body. But our soul keeps our personality intact, and sometimes the baggage attaches to that.

With many prayers and much convincing, we walked Adelbert to the gates of heaven, all the while disconnecting the cords that Helga had so tightly secured from him to her, and her to him in trade. He stepped into the arms of his long awaited family on the other side. More work had to be done, but it would be worth it.

His in-between was lonely. He showed me himself standing beside Helga, begging for her to let him be free. If he ever felt enslaved by life's tragedies, it didn't hold up to death.

Although Adelbert was misunderstood, mostly by himself, he could have a fresh start on the other side if he allowed it to happen. He could burn the baggage so his flight was easier, and he could reconcile with the family that he felt had hurt him and not loved him like he needed. And then face how he raised his kids similarly to the way he was raised, the way he didn't much like being treated, and the reason why he tried to quiet the hurt with alcohol. There was work, but that work would best be done with heaven's help.

That November day in the cemetery cemented a bond that Chuck, Cindi, Mick, and I have kept ever since. It was Adelbert who helped to create a soul connection with two families who would become best friends, that which we lovingly refer to as The Core 4. We've celebrated, we've mourned, we've traveled, we've laughed, and we've laughed even more. I don't believe in coincidences; instead I believe that somehow this was all divinely orchestrated—with a happy ending for all involved, all thanks to Adelbert.

Chapter Seventeen

A Vintage Find

I love the vintage (farmhouse) design, but being an empath I have a hard time going to salvage and antique shops. Just entering a shop that holds items owned by others, attending estate sales or yard sales would leave me overwhelmed and sad. There have been times, even before walking in the door, I've felt like crying or I started uncontrollably shaking. Instead of leaving with a find, I'd leave with a headache and feel pure exhaustion as if I ran a marathon.

Items hold energy of the past owner, especially those objects that have an emotional connection such as jewelry and furniture. Picking up the emotions from objects or having blips of visions after being in the presence, touching, or holding an item is called psychometry, but for me it can be one big emotional distress.

When we moved into our 1930-ish farmhouse I had a vision in my mind how I wanted it decorated. Sure, we had furniture already and I wasn't pitching (or could afford to pitch) all the old and replace with new, or vintage new, but I was determined to add some vintage pieces to my everyday living, both at home and my work office. It just so happens that the area we moved to doesn't lack for these types of shops, and so I decided to work on amping-up my protection of my energy even more so than normal, reading the items to get a sense of if it was okay to bring them home, and energetically cleansing the items once they became ours.

Vintage shopping has become an activity that both my husband and I discovered we both enjoy, as long as it doesn't take up too much energy! While I like more of the shabby chic and repurposed pieces, my husband looks for more nostalgic pieces that remind him of his childhood. More times than not we are off in separate areas browsing, and there have been instances that no matter what I do to protect myself I simply can't deal with the energy of the location or the merchandise the store has. It has zilch effect on Chuck so I'll wait in the car or move on to another shop until he's done. No use making myself ill or taking Chuck's fun away because of my sensitive psychic side.

Some of our vintage finds have been a dining table and chairs, some end tables, signs, bird houses, candle holders, shelves, a couple lamps, and some other miscellaneous pieces that we want to repurpose our self for the garden. The other week we decided to take a drive to a location we'd never been to and it is there that this story really begins.

Chuck gravitated to the potato chip can right away and held it up like it was a newborn baby. I made a face at him, but he explained that his mom had that same chip can in their breezeway when he was growing up.

"She kept bird seed in it," he told me. "I've been looking for one of these for a long time." He sighed and set the New Era Chip can back in its place.

It was just a few dollars, and to me it looked like a rusty can, but to him it was nostalgic. Next to the can was a lamp made out of a yarn spool. To everyone else it probably looked ridiculous, but to me it reminded me of my mom who had collected spools.

The location had a nice energy to it, except at one point I got super dizzy and had to catch myself.

"A portal?" Chuck whispered to me.

He knew how my psychic signs turn into physical signs. I shook my head no. I didn't know why I was all of a sudden feeling out of sorts.

"Probably just hungry," I told him.

I paid the owner and we headed back home with our finds, except Chuck decided to get a car wash and made a turn down another street where we found another vintage shop. This store was more of Chuck's taste, except with a lot of added dust and mildew smelling items. I did find a 1970 eagle statue that my dad had been looking for, and Chuck found a Sinclair Oil sign. His grandpa, who pretty much raised him, worked for Sinclair Oil so anything Sinclair was super special to him. It was a place where the energy was swirling and I simply felt like I needed to get out quick.

It was that night when strange things started happening. Now let me preface this: strange things seem to always happen around me, and we've had some paranormal encounters at the new home, but this was different.

Sitting on the couch that night, both Chuck and I were reading, the house still, and my dad sound asleep in his room, we began to hear footsteps running up and down the stairway.

"Stop it," Chuck called out thinking it was the cats playing chase, only the cats were sound asleep nearby. "That's odd," he said, realizing nobody was there. "Maybe the heat's contracting."

I just nodded in agreement, not thinking anything overly odd, but as soon as we went to bed the footsteps on the stairway began again. They felt rushed, and in a panic, and after getting up several times with nobody there, I put the blankets over my head and fell asleep.

The next night the footsteps started again.

"Why can't you see them?" Chuck asked me, but I didn't have a good answer. I typically saw spirits like flesh and blood, but I was not seeing at all.

I awoke that night to a man and a woman having a conversation from what sounded like our attic. Just above our bedroom we have a large attic that you can actually stand up in and when you walk on the floor boards it makes a distinct noise. The pacing and whispering lasted for almost an hour and it was only a few words that I could make out, but the emotion was again of panic and fear.

Chuck sleeps with ear plugs, so he was confused why dark circles had formed under my eyes that morning.

"Why are they here?" he asked me.

But I didn't know.

The next night I woke up to the same pacing in our attic, up and down our stairway, and then the conversation was closer and more audible.

"We have to hide it," the woman said with a quiet shrill to her voice. "We have to hide it in a safe place until we're ready to go."

Now I was intrigued. Hide what? Who were they hiding it from? Who were they? And what were they doing in my house and why?

The next night Roberta, or Bertie as she asked to be called, shared her story with me.

But why was she there? It was all Chuck's fault. Or that's the story I'm using.

Roberta wore her brown hair pinned back. Her charcoal colored dress was loose fitting around her petite structure and she looked even more drowned out by the black cardigan sweater belted around her waist.

"Do you know where you are?" I asked her.

Her hazel eyes wide, and a bit wild. Not because she could see me, or I her, but because she was scared and that was evident by the way she shivered.

"At the Durant," she whispered back to me.

"The Durant," I tried racking my brain, but I had no idea what she was talking about. She was confident in her response, so I decided to continue with the questioning.

"What are you running from? Can I maybe help you?"

I didn't want to share with her quite yet that she was dead, as obviously she didn't know.

With the ability to hold a conversation with her she wasn't residual energy either, she was intelligent, yet she was stuck in her time and possibly re-living her own demise. It was something that had to be handled delicately.

"Who's with you?"

"Nobody," she quickly answered.

"See, I don't believe you because you were talking to someone about hiding something from someone else."

Bertie stared at me, obviously hoping I'd just go away.

"I promise I want to help you and I won't hurt you."

But Bertie wasn't having anything to do with my promises, and when she stepped away she disappeared.

"Let's try this sleep thing again," I muttered to myself as I climbed back into bed.

Glancing over at Chuck who was sound asleep and snoring, I sighed loudly with some resentfulness and put the pillow over my head. It was all of just a few minutes later when I felt a touch on my arm.

"I've been trying to save money to go away," Bertie confessed to me after I got out of bed and sleepily made my way back to my home office where I wouldn't disturb Chuck.

"Away where?"

Bertie's eyes swelled with tears. "Anywhere, really. Anywhere I won't be found. We won't be found," she corrected.

This time Bertie wasn't alone. She had a young boy with her, about six or seven years of age. His hair was a mess of dark curls and his eyes cornflower blue. Every so often he would peek shyly around Bertie with interest.

"He beats you both, doesn't he? He beats you," I repeated making it more a known statement rather than a question.

It was then that I realized what happened and why they were both stuck, but Bertie decided to trust me enough to share the details.

Her husband was a high profiled union leader, with possible ties to some underground business dealings to boot. Gerald was born soon after their marriage, but with features that didn't favor either of them, and her husband accused her of having an affair.

"He never believed Geri was his from the beginning, but he was. I never cheated. Never."

I believed her. Bertie never cheated, but her husband certainly had his share of girls.

"He thought I didn't know. Women know," Bertie smirked.

Yes, women certainly knew the signs of cheating.

"And then I saw him go into the Flint Tavern Hotel with another woman. He was hand in hand with her, smiling and happy, and I was done."

Bertie could turn her cheek on being cheated on, hit and abused, but she wasn't fine with Geri being hit and abused. Her husband would give her grocery money and she would take a small part of the money and put it away each week. For several years she hid away the little amount of money she could in a potato chip can high on a shelf in her pantry.

He wanted her to come to a corporate celebration in Flint, Michigan at the Durant Hotel.

"He wanted his peers to see him as a family man," Bertie explained. "I packed the potato chip container with the money and when he was in a meeting Geri and I were going to find the train station and leave."

I looked at Bertie hard because I had a strong feeling that we were nearing where I could help, and I was afraid of what her reaction would be once she had the realization.

"Bertie, you didn't make it to the train station, did you?"

"No," she whispered. "He found the money and asked me what I was doing. I told him I was saving to buy him a nice birthday present, but he didn't believe my lie."

"Do you remember after that?"

Bertie stayed silent for what felt like forever before answering.

"He killed us, didn't he?" she flatly said as she absently tousled Geri's curls.

I nodded grimly.

"Do you notice that my clothes are different than yours? And outside looks different? Our cars are different? This is 2017. What year do you think it is?"

Bertie paled. "We're ..."

Bertie and Gerald had been murdered in a fit of blinded rage by the very man who promised to take care of her until death.

Bertie shared that she remembered a funeral, not realizing it was her own and her sons. "I've been wandering with my son, hiding all this time from my husband."

"I think it's time for you to stop hiding and enjoy your heaven," I suggested. "I can help if you'd like me to."

Bertie nodded. She touched my hand with hers. I couldn't help but shiver thinking of how many others are stuck in the in-between, unaware that there is more. But then again, there's many living and breathing people here who aren't living either, stuck in the in-between within their physical bodies.

As I helped the mother and son see the light from the other side, reassuring her that she was a good person and deserved peace, I collapsed back into bed, exhausted.

The next morning the dark circles were even darker around my eyes.

"You okay?" Chuck asked after noticing my exhaustion after a dozen yawns.

"Just tired," I confessed. "And it's all your fault."

Chuck grabbed a cup of dog food and poured it into the dogs' food bowls before answering. "My fault? Why my fault?" Chuck continued to do his chores as we chatted.

"You brought home a ghost," I informed him.

Chuck turned on his heels and looked at me to see if I was serious. I was.

"Wait, how is this my fault again?"

"What did you buy recently?" I jested.

Chuck had no idea what I was referring to until I pointed to the chip tin.

"Oh my gosh, Kristy. I'm so sorry. Do we need to throw it away? We can if we need to. I don't know if I even opened it. Did I open it?"

I laughed in response. "Honey, it's not like a genie popped out of it. A spirit, or spirits actually, were attached to it and I took care of it all."

Chuck looked relieved. "Well, I don't know. I'm new to this world!"

He wasn't new to this world at all, but I let it slide.

"I never thought that a chip tin would have a spirit attached to it. That's a stupid thing to be attached to," Chuck commented.

It wasn't that Bertie was emotionally attached to the tin, it was what she put in the tin that represented freedom to her, and ironically the freedom due to death didn't even happen until Chuck's purchase when I was able to help Bertie and Geri cross over.

"You know, I don't think I ever opened it. Maybe there's money in it," Chuck said spending a minute or two lifting off the rusted lid. "Nope. Nothing in there," he sadly shared, shaking the tin upside down.

Maybe we were supposed to buy the tin after all. Not just to put bird seed in it, but to set free two souls who'd been stuck, hiding from the heaven that they deserved to be in. Even so, I still love vintage finds and antique stores, but I'm hoping to take a break from bringing home the ghosts.

Vintage shopping has always been a thing, but the last couple years it's taken on new life. Whether country road antique markets, weekend pop up boutiques, or an online flea market, the business of used items seems to be a hot commodity and not slowing down anytime soon. For those in tune to energy, though, it can spell a number of disasters, and that isn't always the price tag.

Objects hold energy, and near and dear objects can hold the energy of the last owner(s), or the energy of the environment/circumstance. A few months back a client came home with a beautiful vintage ruby ring from a boutique and for the next two weeks couldn't get out of bed. She had symptoms that her physician couldn't figure out and depression that wasn't her typical personality. When she posted her frustration on Facebook I asked her if she had recently made a vintage purchase (her and I belonged to several vintage buy groups) and sure enough she realized that she brought the ring home just a few days before becoming ill. After some detective work she found out the last owner had passed away from stomach cancer soon after her husband passed away from a heart attack. Had she taken on the energy of the owner? She was assured that was in fact what happened. After she cleansed the ring, and then her house, lo and behold her symptoms and her depression dissipated. Coincidence? Some may say it was, but she's not sure.

A friend of mine purchased a used living room set from a friend of a friend who were getting a divorce and doing an overhaul of their household items. As soon as they placed the couch into the space, she and her husband began arguing almost immediately, and the arguments continued until she decided to smudge her house, paying careful attention to the furniture.

Negative attachments are real. Energies that are in sync help to make life tick by pleasantly, while energies out of whack can make things feel less than stellar. So whether it is furniture, jewelry, clothing, a vase, or whatever else you may find that catches your eye, there are ways to cleanse it so that you lessen your chances of negative energy.

Conclusion

Every time I see the sunrise, hear a child laugh, or feel the wind caress my cheek, I'm reminded that there is much more than the moment I'm in. The bird's sing, the butterfly flutters, morning glories grow, and the world continues to move at its rapid pace. Yet when a loss happens everything feels as if it stands still. It's hard to remember that life continues and can become more fulfilling afterward.

I often wonder through my discussions with spirit if what we miss in this lifetime is what we call patience, which often brings us peace.

There's a legend about a New York City taxi driver who went to pick up an elderly lady, a small woman in her nineties. Wearing a print dress, and veiled pillbox hat, carrying a small suitcase. Her apartment was mostly empty and what was there was covered with sheets. It was his last pick up before the end of his shift and he really just wanted to go home.

Her destination route didn't need to go downtown, but she asked the driver if he could drive her that way. Despite it being a longer commute and more expensive, she shared that she was on her way to hospice, to die. She didn't have very long, she told the driver, and no family left, but she wasn't in a hurry to die either. The cab driver, fighting back tears, shut off the meter and drove her around for several hours. The whole while the elderly lady reminisced and shared the tales of her younger years, the place of her first job, where she went dancing, and where her and her husband had once lived.

After a couple hours the lady grew tired and asked to be taken to her destination. As they traveled in silence, the sun dropped below the horizon. Immediately upon pulling up the lady was met by orderlies to take her to her room. As she reached in her purse to pay, he simply asked if he could have a hug, of which she happily obliged. Her door was shut as she was quickly wheeled away, and he realized that was the sound of the end of her life. The taxi driver couldn't help but wonder how much he might've missed in life while rushing as much as he had.

We're conditioned to think life moments have to be huge and breathtaking, and yet it is every day moments that are gifted to us and are just as special, if not more.

As your days wind down with the sunshine and you welcome in the darkness, you might feel broken and that you can't go on anymore. You may be missing someone or you might be feeling lonely. You might be in pain, physically or psychologically. You might feel misunderstood or lost. Whatever it is that you are going through, I want to remind you to be kind to yourself. To be patient. To find every day moments in life that make you feel alive. Whatever tried to break you—well, it takes time to rebuild, but you can and you will rebuild. Be careful with looking back (you aren't going that way). I hope you lay your head down to sleep believing that something amazing is going to happen. And you've got this even when you don't think you do.

I often speak of how much I love my job. Although I love helping others, the biggest reason I love it is because as I help make the connections to the other side, the other side has no prejudice. Those on the other side don't care how much money you have. They don't care about color of skin, religious preferences, or whether you're straight or gay. There aren't labels like we have here. You can't hide your true self on the other side. Your soul and spirit is transparent and alive, more alive than we are here on the earth. The soul, which means life and the spirit, the true core of who you are, is the center of spiritual and emotional experiences, and all it wants is to feed itself with love.

We all have choices here whether we feed the negative or spread the love. We have those same choices when we cross over. We each have an ability to shine our light into the darkness and dismiss the shadows or get caught up in absorbing the anger of the world. You are deserving of a heavenly state of mind which can turn into a heavenly ever after. Where there's a will there's a way. Where's there's hate there will be more, but there is always more love; know that you are deserving of that.

Everyone's life is riddled with mistakes, chaos, and regrets, but often that is a one-way ticket to anywhere but heaven. There's always action that you can do to stop doing what you're doing, or allow what's happening to you to stop happening.

We all will mourn and grieve at least once in our lifetime. We all do it differently. We all have taken moments for granted, thinking there would be a later, a tomorrow, a next week. If death has taught us anything, it's to love—to speak the love—because there are no guarantees. And when it's our own time to cross over, remember that you have a choice here to find your heaven, hell, or in-between, just as much as you do in spirit. I'd like to think the choice is an easy one.

Appendix

Ways to Cleanse the Energy

- **Smudging:** Hold the burning sage or cedar stick and with its smoke ask that all negative energy be removed.
- **Moonlight:** Preferably during the full moon, place your object under the moonlight and ask that it cleanse the energy.
- **Sunlight:** Same as moonlight, but for the sun.
- **Sea Salt:** Place sea salt around your object and ask that all of the negative energy be absorbed into the salt.
- **Earth:** Bury your object in the dirt (or flower pot)—just make sure to put a marker where you put them. My least favorite cleanse, but it can help with jewelry. After you've buried your objects ask God/Goddess/spirits of nature to cleanse and renew.
- **Sacred Breath:** Call on your higher self, guides, and guardians and blow away the negativity off the object (like blowing out your birthday candle).

- **Cool Water:** Wash the object with cool water and sea salt, but make certain the points of the object are facing down the drain to run the negative energy right down the sink. Not everything can be washed, so make sure it is okay to be cleansed this way. I have used this technique with clothing. I've also utilized holy water and rose water.

- **Visualize:** Hold or touch your object and visualize it being cleansed by your guides and angels.

- **Crystals:** You can place crystals on or around the objects to help cleanse. Selenite, blue kyanite, citrine, snowflake obsidian, and black tourmaline are some of my favorites and can absorb negative energy. Just make sure to smudge or rinse off the crystals with sea salt water afterward.

- **Essential Oils:** I do love my essential oils, and I've made my share of sprays with essential oils and herbs and washed my objects with this (although you can diffuse them as well). You can add a pinch of sea salt, and even crush up some crystals with it. Simply use your own intuition and positive intention when creating.

  - **Rose**—Helps to raise the vibration of the energy

  - **Peppermint**—Uplifts and calms energy

  - **Basil**—A protective oil

  - **Cypress**—Grounds and protects

  - **Lavender**—A great neutralizer and helps relax

  - **Frankincense**—Cleanses the aura of people and objects

  - **Sage**—Clears the negative energy and neutralizes

- **Palo Santo**—Known as holy wood, helps to protect, cleanse, and remove negative energy
- **Cinnamon**—Relaxes tense energy
- **Cedarwood**—Connects us to angels and allows them to help cleanse

Whatever cleansing you utilize, though, it works best with intention and with prayer. Positive brings more positive. *"Disintegrate all negative energies, thoughts, and emotions from this room/object now. Fill this space with love, blessings, and joy from above."*

Before taking on a vintage purchase I do try to spend some time holding it, touching it, and just sensing it. If I get the "stay away" feeling, I trust in that even if it's beautiful. And if you bring home something that had been hibernating with negative energy know that you more than likely don't have to toss it or call it a loss, instead simply try one of the above solutions.

The Cross Over

Protect Yourself—You want to make sure that you are speaking to a spirit of the white light (someone that is good and not a prankster). I say a prayer of protection asking my guides and protectors to assist me by surrounding me and the spirit with loving and protective energy.

Make Sure—Make certain this is what the spirit wants. You can't force anyone to go to the other side. So simply ask if this is their request. If you feel a heavy feeling, that could indicate that they aren't ready. A lighter feeling would be a green light to go. Remember that they are a person with feelings and fear too. Don't demand; have compassion. Since there is no such thing as time and space in the spirit world, the spirits can be trapped, or earthbound, for hundreds to thousands of years. Especially if I feel a heavy feeling, I will tell them what year it is and let them know that they aren't living their highest purpose by wandering, and then I check in again to see if they've changed their opinion.

Bring in Their Family—I close my eyes and visualize a brilliant white light coming down from the sky and encompassing them with love and comfort. It is a pathway of invitation. I walk with them as close to the light as I can, and I point out the souls, their family members and friends, on the other side who want to help them over the threshold. If they decide not to cross, you can tell them that they are no longer welcome to be around you. Like a baby blanket to a toddler, they may not realize that giving it up is a good thing until they realize they can't have it.

The Send Off—I offer a hand to those in the white light and visualize them crossing. If you do not see or hear anything, don't worry, simply pay attention to how you and the energy around you feels.

Extra Help—Sometimes cross overs require a dose of extra help. I typically ask for angels and guides to assist, and will specifically call on Archangel Michael and Archangel Azrael. Michael has a blue sword that can cut ties to this earthly plane and Azrael is the angel of death and dying and provides comfort. He is often seen with twinkling yellow energy. I also ask my guides and family members on the other side to assist in welcoming the new soul or souls.

Final Release—I always keep the door open for a brief second and ask if any other wandering souls would like to cross over and join the party.

Close the Door—Once I feel all the spirits that decide to cross, I visualize the light dimming and the door closing. I then ask the angels to seal the doorway so nobody can cross back into this plane and I thank everyone heavenly and earthly who assisted.

Shields Up

Before every paranormal investigation, I pray. Before going into a cemetery, whether for an investigation or to care for a loved one's grave, I pray. Before going into a hospital or funeral home, I pray. It isn't obvious; you can do it in your head, although I wouldn't care if it was. But it can be said in your head or out loud. It is effective just the same.

I don't believe there is a wrong or a right thing to say. Being raised Lutheran, my prayers are often to what most refer to as God or the Lord. I ask for assistance and protection from the archangels, especially Archangel Michael, my own guides, and my loved ones on the other side. I typically will ask for the white light of God to surround me and protect me, and then say a prayer of release when I'm leaving said establishments, making certain that nothing uninvited hitches a ride home.

Note that if you are not comfortable calling on God, you can ask for angels, Saints, spirits of nature, or whatever/whomever resonates with your faith.

What is white light? White light is strong protection from the Divine and acts like a brick wall, protecting you from lower and toxic energies. It is your spiritual sword.

It can be dangerous to go into a location without the right tools, that includes protection of your own true self.

Sample Prayers

The Lord's Prayer: Our Father in heaven, hallowed be your name. Your kingdom come, your will be done, on earth as it is in heaven. Give us this day our daily bread, and forgive us our debts, as we also have forgiven our debtors. And lead us not into temptation, but deliver us from evil. Amen.

Prayer for Strength: We ask for strength from God and ask that Archangel Michael raise up his sword to defend us from all evil and negativity, protecting us from all evil and negativity. We ask for the white light to surround us with love. We ask that all negative energies and lost souls be taken into the light and freed according to God's will, and that we are blessed as we do your work with love and ethics. May your will be done. Amen.

Circle of White Light: I ask that God, my archangels, guides, and past loved ones surround me with a perfect and holy white light and that it protects me throughout my journey today. I ask that only positive and high vibrational energies are allowed through and that everything I say and do is with unconditional love and peace. Surround my friends and family in the circle of protection, if it be their will. In His name I pray. Amen.

Release: I ask that God, the archangels, and my guides remove and release any and all toxic, negative, or unhealthy energy that may be attached. I ask that you cut the cords and that they return nevermore. I ask that all negative attachments, influences, and dark energies be removed from my body and all my properties. Fill up every cell in my body, mind, and spirit with the highest of white lights so I can share love and peace. Amen.

References

Alexander, Eban. *Proof of Heaven: A Neurosurgeon's Journey into the Afterlife.* New York: Simon & Schuster, 2012.

Byrd, Cathy. *The Boy Who Knew Too Much: An Astounding True Story of a Young Boy's Past-Life Memories.* Carlsbad, CA: Hay House, Inc., 2017.

Griswold, R.W. "Death of Edgar A. Poe." *New York Daily Tribune*, vol. IX, no. 156, October 9, 1849.

Grunwald, Lisa, and Stephen J. Adler. *Letters of the Century: America, 1900-1999.* New York: Dial Press, 1999.

Neal, Mary C. *To Heaven and Back: A Doctor's Extraordinary Account of Her Death, Heaven, Angels, and Life Again: A True Story.* Colorado Springs, CO: Waterbook Press, 2012.

Nerbern, Kent. *Make Me an Instrument of Your Peace: Living in the Spirit of the Prayer of Saint Francis.* New York: HarperOne,1999.

Rabin, Andrew. "Bede, Dryhthelm, and the Witness to the Other World: Testimony and Conversion in the Historia ecclesiastica," *Modern Philology* 106, no. 3 (February 2009): 375-398.

Willingham, AJ. "This May Be the Most Brutal, Honest Obituary Ever." *CNN*. Accessed February 13, 2017. https://www.cnn.com/2017/02/13/health/obituary-charping-texas-man-trnd/index.html

About the Author

Kristy Robinett is a psychic medium and author from Michigan who began seeing spirits at the age of three. When she was eight, the spirit of her deceased grandfather helped her escape from a would-be kidnapper, and it was then that Robinett realized the other side wasn't so far away. As an adult, she was often called upon by the local police department to examine cold cases in a new light and from a different angle. She gained a solid reputation for being extremely accurate at psychical profiling and giving new perspectives on unsolved crimes. It was then that she began working with a variety of law enforcement agencies, attorneys, and private investigators around the United States, aiding in missing persons, arson, and cold cases, and in 2014 appeared on a one-hour special on the Investigation Network (ID) called *Restless Souls*, spotlighting a police case she assisted on.

Robinett teaches psychic development and paranormal investigating at local colleges, lectures across the country, and is a regular media commentator. She is the author of *Tails from the Afterlife: Stories of Signs, Messages, and Inspiration from your Companion Animals*; *Messages From a Wonderful Afterlife: Signs Loved Ones Send from Beyond*; *It's a Wonderful Afterlife*; *Forevermore: Guided in Spirit by Edgar Allan Poe*; *Messenger Between Worlds: True Stories from a Psychic Medium*; *Higher Intuitions Oracle*; *Ghosts of Southeast Michigan*; and *Michigan's Haunted Legends and Lore*.

Kristy Robinett is a wife and mom to four adult children and several animals. She enjoys gardening, cooking, exploring old country towns, porch sitting, and graveyards. In 2016 she and her husband bought their dream farmhouse in rural Michigan.

You can visit her online at KristyRobinett.com, facebook.com/kristyrobinett, or Twitter.com/kristyrobinett.

STORIES OF SIGNS, MESSAGES & INSPIRATION
FROM YOUR ANIMAL COMPANIONS

TAILS

from the

AFTERLIFE

KRISTY ROBINETT

Tails from the Afterlife
*Stories of Signs, Messages & Inspiration
from your Animal Companions*
KRISTY ROBINETT

Even when their physical bodies are gone, your beloved pets live on in spirit and in their undying devotion to you. *Tails from the Afterlife* shares amazing and inspiring stories of the signs, symbols, and messages that your pets send, proving that they're waiting for you and even helping you from the other side.

From near-death experiences to witness accounts to life-saving tails—pun intended—Kristy Robinett will have you both crying and laughing as she presents an array of animals and their heavenly hellos. This comforting book also offers suggestions for dealing with grief and guidance on how to make the connection with your deceased companion.

978-0-7387-5217-4, 240 pp., 5¼ x 8   **$16.99**

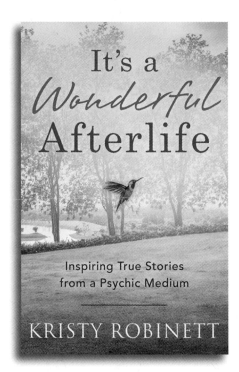

It's a
Wonderful
Afterlife

Inspiring True Stories
from a Psychic Medium

KRISTY ROBINETT

It's a Wonderful Afterlife
Inspiring True Stories from a Psychic Medium
KRISTY ROBINETT

Ever since she was a child, psychic medium Kristy Robinett has communicated with spirits who have shared their experiences of death and what happens afterwards. In this collection of heart-warming stories that answer the most common questions about the afterlife, Robinett delves into the nature of heaven, if there is a hell, and what the transition to the other side is like. With personal experiences and stories from clients, Kristy explores the many signs and symbols that our loved ones share with us to assure that it is, indeed, a wonderful afterlife.

978-0-7387-4073-7, 240 pp., 5³⁄₁₆ x 8   **$15.99**

Messenger *between* Worlds

True Stories from a Psychic Medium

Kristy Robinett

Messenger Between Worlds
True Stories from a Psychic Medium
KRISTY ROBINETT

At the age of three, Kristy Robinett predicted her grandmother's death. When she was eight, the spirit of her deceased grandfather helped her escape from a would-be kidnapper. This captivating, powerful memoir is filled with unforgettable scenes: spot-on predictions, countless spirit visits at home and school, menacing paranormal activity, and Kristy's first meeting with two spirit guides who became her constant allies. Born into a strict religious family, Kristy believed she was cursed and hid her psychic abilities for many years. Over time, she learned to use her talent to do good in the world, and now she has decided to share her incredible story. Follow Kristy's emotional journey through a difficult childhood, stormy marriages, conflict with faith, job loss, and illness—and the hard-won lessons that opened her heart to true love and acceptance of her unique gift.

978-0-7387-3666-2, 288 pp., 5³⁄₁₆ x 8   **\$14.99**

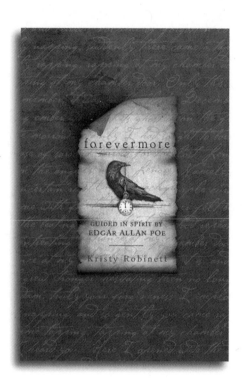

Forevermore
Guided in Spirit by Edgar Allan Poe
KRISTY ROBINETT

Kristy Robinett has always had helpers in spirit, but when she was thirteen, she met the most fascinating spirit guide of all—Edgar Allan Poe. *Forevermore* tells the true story of how Edgar Allan Poe helped Kristy fulfill her destiny as a writer and a psychic medium.

Far from being a madman (as he's often portrayed in the media), Poe is an insightful guide and a sleuth with a passion for justice. Working with law enforcement, Kristy and Poe uncover truths of the past—murders, suicides, missing persons—and shed light on the wrongs that have found their way into the present day.

Join Kristy as she shows how personal growth can come from the unlikeliest places and affirms the comforting fact that we are all given the chance to learn and evolve on the other side.

978-0-7387-4067-6, 240 pp., 5³⁄₁₆ x 8   **$15.99**
